"Carlos has written a book about the mind and heart of humans, drawing on many years of dedicated study of the earth wisdom teachings. His insights come from engaging with the ancient teachings and testing them in his own life, and there is honesty and wisdom in his words."

— CHRIS LÜTTICHAU, author of *Calling Us Home*

"As Audrey Lourdes famously said: 'The master's tools will never dismantle the master's house.' That's why Extinction Rebellion asked us to say no to an extractive, exploitative, life-destroying system, by creating a regenerative culture. But what does this mean in practice? Carlos Glover is offering us a meaningful contribution towards the cultures we need to remember. Here is a rich compendium of teachings and practices, based in ancient wisdom, to sustain, inspire, and grow us, as we find our way back home together."

— GAIL BRADBROOK, Ph.D., co-founder of Extinction Rebellion

"The time is right. Carlos takes us beyond a narcissistic view of ourselves to one that enables us to be more functional. This book goes beyond self-help to the birthing of a new world and gives a framework to how we move there. I thought it was excellent. "

— CAMERON BROUGHTON, founder of Journeys with Soul

"Carlos has written a book that is simple, easy to grasp, eminently practical, and deceptively deep. Its teachings come from a well-digested journey, and they reflect the man: kind, committed, and just. Carlos has followed the road of soul, meeting shadow and light with equanimity and strength, and he invites us to do the same. He blends the challenges of crisis with the beauty that life gives. I am glad to recommend this book, hewn from the rock of direct experience. Enjoy, and let's get down to work."

— YA'ACOV DARLING KHAN, bestselling author of *Jaguar in the Body, Butterfly in the Heart* and *Shaman*

"Carlos has really thought it all through and assembled this book with stories and reminiscences so it touches many levels at the same time. It is a beautiful piece of work with charm, grace, and a gentle persistence in teaching the Medicine way of seeing the world."

— LEO RUTHERFORD, founder of Eagle's Wing Centre for Contemporary Shamanism

"This wonderful book guides us through the eight directions of the Medicine Wheel, where we learn about actualizing our 'unlimited potential.' Reading it is like participating in a psycho-spiritual vision quest. The book is full of wise words, which are skilfully woven into a transformative narrative, inviting us to restore a deeper sense of wholeness. "

— MICK COLLINS, Ph.D., author of *Visionary Spirit*

"So many years of study and insight of craft and care. Carlos has created a great gift for humanity . . . it is easy to read yet intriguing and deep. It is clear and precise, balanced with warmth and compassion. It reveals the essence of the Earth teachings in a way that is much needed. It is such an amazing book . . . a great boon to offer to all those on the path of Self-realization."

— RICHARD GOOD, founder of Imaginal Collective

"I love this inspirational book. Guided all the way by Carlos's own experience and humanity, the practices are transformative. It left me feeling powerful, and that I really am doing something useful to help heal the global crisis."

— SIMON SMITH, founder of Heart and Soul Funerals

EARTH WISDOM
TEACHINGS
Practical Guidance from the
Eight Directions of the Medicine Wheel

Carlos Philip Glover

FINDHORN PRESS

Findhorn Press
One Park Street
Rochester, Vermont 05767
www.findhornpress.com

Findhorn Press is a division of Inner Traditions International

Revised and expanded edition of *Earth Wisdom for Our Global Crisis*, originally published in the United Kingdom in 2023 by Earth Wisdom Teachings

Disclaimer
The information in this book is given in good faith and intended for information only. Neither author nor publisher can be held liable by any person for any loss or damage whatsoever which may arise directly or indirectly from the use of this book or any of the information therein.

Cataloging-in-Publication Data for this title is available from the Library of Congress

ISBN 979-8-88850-163-4 (print)
ISBN 979-8-88850-164-1 (ebook)

Printed and bound in India by Nutech Print Services

10 9 8 7 6 5 4 3 2 1

Illustrations by Carlos Philip Glover
Cover Illustration "Sacred Twenty Count" by Angele Camus, angele.art
Edited by Nicky Leach
Text design and layout by Damian Keenan
This book was typeset in Adobe Garamond Pro, Calluna Sans and Akaya Kanadaka with ITC Century Std Book Condensed used as a display typeface.

To send correspondence to the author of this book, mail a first-class letter to the author c/o Inner Traditions • Bear & Company, One Park Street, Rochester, VT 05767, USA and we will forward the communication, or contact the author directly at **www.carlosphilipglover.com**

This Book

is dedicated to the

evolutionary unfolding

of our collective consciousness.

Let us find our way back into

wholeness and ecological

balance with Self,

Life and Earth.

Contents

CONCLUSION

A donation of the author's income from this book will go to Ehama Institute, New Mexico, and to Survival International to support the rights of threatened tribal people.

Preface

An epiphany is a sudden breakthrough in consciousness. It is an evolutionary leap that expands our awareness of the essential nature of life, a revelation leading to fresh realization about the Self and Universe. It often brings a profound sense of inner peace and a change in lifestyle. An epiphany is an experience that's impossible to ignore and available to everyone.

This book is dedicated to the evolution of human consciousness. Such a quantum leap is possible and needed, and we are being called to it. It will bring harmony to our relationships and enable us to restore ecological balance to the earth.

Our global crisis has many symptoms, but its underlying cause and solution are within us. We can see the crisis in many areas; for example the climate, extinction, diversity, society, politics, finance, and international relations. But whatever form it takes, the remedy needs to include a shift in our consciousness. When we come into a new relationship with ourselves, we are better able to meet the challenges in our world and produce favourable results. For the human journey to continue it is vital that we make this shift.

Earth Wisdom Teachings is the result of nearly 40 years of study and learning. My journey began after a personal crisis that turned out to be a break*through* rather than a break*down*. I changed my direction in life and started environmental campaigning and personal development. I had two essential questions: How can we heal ourselves, and how can we heal our relationship with the planet? While holding these questions in my heart I realized that they are interdependent—we can't do one without the other.

On my quest for healing, I came across many useful teachings and tools. I discovered an ancient tradition of Earth Wisdom that flourished among the Maya and Toltec civilizations and has touched people of many cultures. Over time, I came to see that this body of teachings has the power to unlock our unlimited potential. It can create conditions that encourage epiphany. It has provided the compass and map for my own voyage of self-discovery, and it informs much of what is in this book.

However, this is *not* an invitation to adopt a new ideology. This way of learning is not a dogma. It is more like an orchard in which anyone can gather the fruit of self-knowledge. It is about awakening consciousness. Whatever your beliefs and practices, this consciousness is already within you.

I recognize my privilege as a white male living in a time and place in which it is possible to follow this way without persecution. I offer this in honour of those who died keeping this flame of knowledge alive.

This book is decorated with circular designs because it expresses a circular way of seeing and being. There are many natural circles on Earth, and when you notice them you realize that they can teach us about wholeness, harmony, and who we are. If you choose to read on, that's what we're going to explore together.

A very warm welcome to the journey of this book.

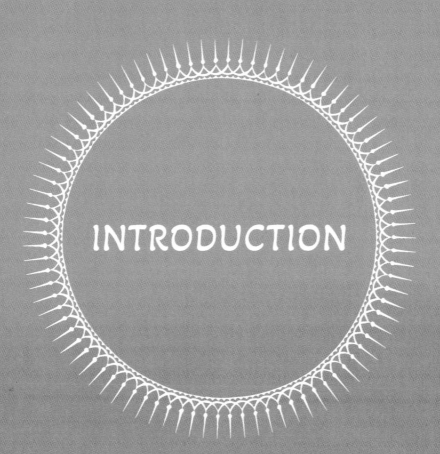

INTRODUCTION

Earth Medicine for Global Evolution

"We need to talk about the next step of evolution. That may seem bold, but the time calls for boldness."

The eyes of the old man, my teacher, sparkled as he spoke. They were as blue as the Caribbean Sea in which I'd just been swimming.

"But if you're going to write about Earth Medicine and its effect on human evolution, tell stories."

Those words were the genesis of this book.

"Medicine" in this context comes from a mistranslation. French fur-trappers exploring the backwoods of North America noticed that there were wise people caring for the wellbeing of their tribe. "Who are these people?" they asked. The Native people told them that these wise ones were known as "the Medewyn," which the trappers translated as *medecins,* the French word for "doctors." It is from French, therefore, that this use of the word found its way into English. For Indigenous people, though, "Medicine" means "wholeness and balance." It includes not only your physical health but your mental, emotional, and spiritual wellbeing. Anything can be your Medicine. A pill can be your Medicine, or a walk in the sunshine. A dog, a mouse, or an eagle can help you feel strong. A challenge can put you in touch with your power. A practice could heal you. Or a story might show you something deeper about yourself. All of these could feed your wholeness and balance; Medicine is the power that flows from within.

Our mainstream culture is much more interested in the outer world than the inner. At school, it's rare to learn much about feelings, dreams, or body sensations. We don't study intuition, awareness, or even good communication. We're not taught about thought. It's as if the only thing that matters is matter.

My Medicine teachers taught me that it's as important to care for the inner world as the outer one. Thought matters. How we do things counts as much as what we do. The quality of our inner world—thoughts, feelings, attention, and so on—determines the quality of our relationship with the outer world, and everything in it.

Because of our emphasis on the outer world, our culture is out of balance. When we're out of balance inside, our effect on the outside is out of balance. The interconnected crises we face on our planet arise from our internal world that is out of balance. Yes, we need to change things "out there," but we also need to address the imbalance "in here." To meet our global challenges, we are called to expand our consciousness. But how?

That's the question I want to address.

The Flowering of Human Consciousness

If you walk out on the earth and go somewhere high, such as a hill or mountaintop, you see the horizon all around you. It's a circle where earth meets sky, and you're in the centre of it. If you watch long enough, you'll see the sun rise in the east and set in the west. And if you're in the northern hemisphere, you'll notice the warmth spreading from the South and the cold from the north.

Long ago, our ancestors noticed these and other circles in nature. They sat in silent awe around the fire as the stars moved around the heavens. They saw that the pupils of our eyes are circular. So is our field of vision. Birds make their nests in circles, and many of the old people lived in circular dwellings, such as yurts, teepees, and igloos. They baked bread in circular loaves. And many things in life move in circles—the ebb and flow of tides, the dance of day and night, and the cycle of seasons around the year.

Ancient people learned directly from the elements—earth, air, fire, and water. They wondered at this mysterious Universe, contemplating their relationship with the earth and her other offspring, such as plants and animals. They understood that all of life is relationship: everything is related to everything else. And everything—from stars to stones, rivers to rainbows, and carrots to kangaroos—is one thing, one song, the Universe. Even the unseen world of consciousness is part of the Universe.

Gradually, these insights evolved into wisdom traditions, and people created symbols to express and pass them on to their children. In many places around the planet, people built stone circles. These reflected the circles in nature and were symbols of wholeness and eternity. In the lineage I follow, the earth teachings are arranged in circles or "Medicine Wheels." This helps people think in a holistic way and see their relationship with all of life.

The lineage of the Medicine Wheels has been evolving over thousands of years. For much of that time, it has helped sustain the wholeness and balance of communities that have lived in close relationship with nature.

During the conquest of the Americas, this precious flame of knowledge came close to being extinguished, because many carriers of wisdom were persecuted and slaughtered. It survived in secret on the finest of threads, and in the late 20th century its keepers began to share it with those who were interested. Now it is an influence on the renaissance of spiritual self-awareness that is part of our collective evolution.

On your hill or mountaintop, you might like to build a Medicine Wheel. To the East, you would place a stone to honour the sun, the bringer of light and fire. Opposite, in the West, you'd place another stone for the earth, which gives us form and is the dark within the light. In the South, you would place another stone for plants and water, and in the North a stone for the animals and air. You can stand in the centre and see that you are related to the sun, earth, plants, and animals.

Then you might add a further four stones in the non-cardinal directions: the Southeast for the present; the Southwest for the past; the Northwest for the future; and the Northeast for movement and change. You might then stand in the centre and imagine these eight stones represent aspects of you: in the East, your creative fire; in the West, your physical form; in the South, the growing power of your emotion; and in the North, your mind and heart.

The Medicine Wheel is an ancient design handed down over many generations. It is a sacred circle, a symbol of life, with no beginning and no end. And it is a map to guide us on the journey of self-knowledge. It enables us to become more intimate with the mystery of who we are, and of life. It is not a dogma. It encourages us to question, to follow our self-authority, and to develop in our own unique way.

This book is arranged like a Medicine Wheel, with eight chapters, each about a different part of ourselves. Human consciousness is complex, and this is a way to understand ourselves more deeply. These eight aspects of ourselves are like the petals of a flower, each integral to the whole. Developing one aspect supports the health and vitality of the whole.

It's difficult, if not impossible, to understand consciousness with scientific method, because consciousness isn't independent of us. It's not a thing; we *are* consciousness. Looking for a location for consciousness is like pulling apart a flower to find the source of its beauty. Is it in the petal? Nope. Is it in the stamen? Nope. Stigma? Ovary? No, because beauty isn't just in the eye of the beholder; it's in the relationship between the beholder and the beheld.

The collective consciousness of all humans is like a tree, and each of us is a leaf on one branch. I believe the tree is coming into flower. As each of us awakens, each in our unique way, we add to the flowering of the whole tree. The Medicine Wheel shows us our relationship with the Universe and all its expressions, and all of humanity's wisdom traditions can support this evolutionary movement of consciousness. But it is through experience that we grow in Self-knowledge, and it is through practice that we learn to read our own "book," the book of the Self.

The Form of This Book

The eight chapters of this book are about the eight directions of the Medicine Wheel. Each direction represents a realm of universal consciousness. We access this consciousness with our intelligences. From a Medicine Wheel perspective, "intelligence" is more than intellect and cleverness; it also includes our creativity, presence, emotion, path, healing, dreaming, heart, and energy. All of us have eight innate "intelligences," and we develop them through experience and practice.

My intention is to illuminate these energies with stories and explanations. Each chapter has four sections intended to evoke that realm of consciousness. And each section is followed by a practice designed to awaken the innate wisdom within us.

There are many other practices in schools of consciousness, both ancient and modern. They are technologies of consciousness, techniques for our awakening. But whatever you choose as a practice, it is only a practice if you practise it. Medicine becomes yours if you digest it through experience, not if you only read about it.

As we awaken these realms of consciousness in ourselves, we change the field of our collective consciousness. We're both human individuals and parts of the collective human consciousness, just as a fish is part of a shoal or a bird is part of a flock. As we awaken, we affect the collective consciousness. As we transform the collective consciousness, we shift to ground on which we can effectively resolve the global challenges that confront us.

The journey starts with creation intelligence in the East, where the sun rises. The sequence flows with the movement of the sun clockwise around the Wheel: Southeast, South, Southwest, West, Northwest, North, Northeast. This sequence is a natural flow of energy that takes us into the centre of the Self. It is a spiral journey that deepens our self-knowledge and heightens our connection with the Universe.

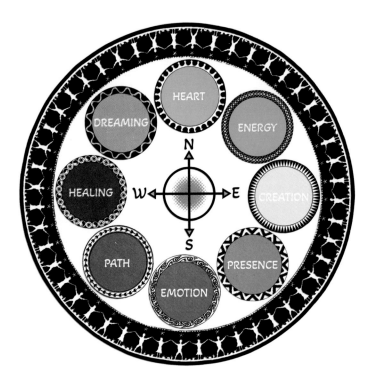

The Eight Directions

My Journey

But how did I come to be speaking with my teacher on a golden beach in the Yucatan in Mexico?

Many of us are drawn to personal development through the urge to heal. What I needed to heal erupted as a teenager. I was bullied at school and had low self-esteem. I didn't tell anyone. Shame made me hide, and I felt desperately alone. I had no idea how to heal my pain or manage my emotional experiences. A few years later my world fell apart, and I had to learn how to rebuild it with solid foundations. I began to do so through counselling, meditation, and an exploration of Buddhism.

In the 1980s, I had canoed into the Amazon and witnessed the devastation caused by oil wells and cattle ranching. This had deeply upset me. It was clear that apart from extinguishing other species we were putting our own survival in jeopardy, and I wondered how we could heal our relationship with nature. I had the idea that Indigenous people might teach us something about this relationship. I felt an affinity with them. After all, some of my happiest memories were of playing in woods and by streams. Then someone suggested joining a journey based on "Earth Medicine." In spite of my conventional background, I felt called and stepped into the unknown.

Thus began my journey back into wholeness. I found that Earth Medicine was a path of not only beauty but also of power—not power "over" other people but personal power that comes from within. It addressed the twin questions of how to heal ourselves and how to restore nature. It was an adventure that challenged me to let go of pretences but nurtured me through relationship with the earth. And after walking this way for a while, I realized that I no longer felt lonely.

I am not Indigenous. My native tongue is one of the dominant languages, English, and my nationality is that of a former imperial power, Britain. I recognize the great harm and hurt that we Europeans have caused as we took over other continents. Along with the genocide and ecocide, colonization has wiped out many Indigenous cultures, and horrible things have been done to their wisdom keepers. I have asked myself: "Who am I, as a privileged person from the dominant culture, to write about the Medicine Wheel?"

I come to this writing with caution, respect, and reverence. And in my heart, I carry the poignant words my teacher's teacher told him: "Breathe these teachings into the world." They said: "It is time, and maybe some good will come of it."

I was brought up to identify with the mainstream culture of industrial consumerism, but I'm aware that in spite of material abundance, something is lacking. For many of us, it's as if there's a hole inside and nothing will fill it. My deepest identity is as a spirit, part of all spirit. I am related with all life. The Medicine Wheel has helped me see this. Though it has been carried by some Indigenous cultures, the Medicine Wheel does not belong to any one people. If anything, it belongs to the earth—as *we* do.

I believe it can help us come back into wholeness and balance so that we no longer need to exploit people or planet.

To heal ourselves and restore our Earth, we need to recover the indigeneity of our soul. It's essential for our salvation as a species—and for all species—that we fall back in love with the beauty and wonder of nature. Recognizing our relationship with all of life is a necessary part of this, and the Medicine Wheel enables us to do so.

By realizing our interrelatedness, we can heal ourselves and begin to restore the delicate web of creation. All things are on the Medicine Wheel, and all things are equal on it. I believe it has the power to influence our collective destiny in a beneficial way, and that's why I'm dedicating this book—and my life—to this healing.

So, after many years of study with various teachers, I came to be training with the old man. We had come to the shores of the Yucatan because it was there that his teachings had flourished long ago among the Maya. We climbed the steps of a pyramid and made a ceremony to honour the lineage of teachings. And each day we took in the blessing of the four elements: Ocean, Sky, Earth, and Sun.

Each morning I would arise early enough to see the last stars fading. I would go onto the beach to watch the golden orb of fire emerge from the waters to the east.

THE EIGHT
DIRECTIONS

1

East: Creation

Einstein said: "A human being is part of the whole called by us Universe, a part limited in time and space. He experiences himself, his thoughts and feelings, as something separated from the rest, a kind of optical delusion of his consciousness. The striving to free oneself from this delusion is the one issue of true religion."[1]

How can we free ourselves? The first step is to awaken to our relationship with the Universe. Whatever we think, we're never truly separate. We are connected with everything else. We are constantly exchanging energy with the rest of the Universe—through our breath, for example. We are in the Universe, and the Universe is in us.

The Medicine Wheel helps us realize this connection. On the Wheel, East is the direction of the sun and stars. When the sun rises in the east, its light awakens us from sleep and we begin our day's journey. It is from here that we begin our journey to the centre.

The sun is our star. It generates life on Earth and shines on everyone unconditionally. Solar energy goes to everyone. So the East is also the direction of life-generating, creative energy, and this life force is in all of us and in all things. The sun is generative and creative, and so are we.

We may think of creativity in terms of the "creative arts"—art, music, drama, and so on—but creation energy goes beyond that; it shines through our words, thoughts, and deeds, especially when our self-expression is free and inspired. The "seat" of this energy in us is the base (first) chakra, the genitals or generative organs (making love can be highly creative!).

Each of us expresses creation in unique ways, but our essence is the essence of all things—we are expressions of the universal life force. When we realize our oneness with the Universe, we expand consciousness. Living from this realization helps heal the global crisis. In this chapter, each section will discuss some ways of doing this.

The Heyoka Joker

The Heyoka Joker shows how to use surprise and humour to break free of limiting assumptions and become free in our self-expression. As we open our mind and spirit, we become more conscious of the field of unlimited potential. This field is the source of the creative life force that sustains us.

Let There Be Light

At the heart of each atom is light. Light is a mystery that fills all things. It is the creative force that animates Life. Without light, there would be no life. It is at the core of each cell in us. We are related to it, even to the light that shines from distant galaxies, and when we become aware of this relationship, we awaken inner peace. Light is Spirit, the essence of creation. We are one.

The Magic of Image-Thought

Imagination is the "being" side of creativity, the side that comes before "doing." It enables us to shape the creative life force as it emanates from the field of unlimited potential into form.

The Way of Ceremony

Creation is the dance of masculine and feminine, and all things in creation have both polarities in them—both the being and becoming. Ceremony is a way to bring these into balance and to receive the spark of creative inspiration.

The Heyoka Joker

Our essential nature is that we are Spirit, part of all Spirit. We are the light of pure consciousness. This light is infinite, brilliant, and free. It is the light of the Universe, the birthing place of unlimited possibility. When we reawaken this luminous essence, we open the field of all potential. This is our first step into creation intelligence. Let's begin this exploration with a story.

A long time ago some people wanted to create a community for personal growth. They found a place in a great forest on the slopes of some high mountains. They made beautiful spaces for music, meditation, and movement; they created a hall, library, and guest house. Outside you could contemplate in the gardens where golden carp swam in ponds. The place was renowned for miles around, and visitors used to come for retreats and workshops.

But gradually things started to slip. Members began to approach their spiritual practices as routine chores and to do them without enthusiasm. They started turning up late for morning practice or sleeping in when the bell called them, and they argued more and more about work. One by one people began to leave, and little by little the buildings fell into disrepair; the roof of the hall started leaking, and there was no money to fix it. The garden was getting overgrown, and the ponds silted up with leaves and mud.

Eventually, there were only a few members left, all of them getting on in years. They hardly had any visitors now and almost nothing in donations. And one of them, the woman they called "the Abbess," worried about how to keep the place running at all, let alone restore the meditation hall. One day she went to ask for guidance from the Unseen Mystery and found wine dregs in the holy chalice and mouse droppings on the altar.

The next day a wandering holy man came out of the forest to visit them. His face was etched with experience and his long hair white with wisdom. He stayed a couple of nights. On the third morning, he was getting ready to leave when the Abbess asked him: "Can you tell me how to keep this place from falling apart?"

The holy man shook his head. "Sorry. I can't think of anything." He started to leave, then said: "But I'll tell you this. The Saviour is living among you!" And with that, he turned and disappeared into the woods.

The Abbess stared after him. The Saviour living among them? And when she told the others they were equally surprised.

"One of us is the Saviour, Messiah, Buddha! Who could it be?" they all wondered. "Could it be Sister So-and-so? She's always on another level. Or Brother So-and-so? He spends a lot of time in his room. Perhaps he's always praying?"

That night they were all on time for evening prayers. Whoever it was, they didn't want to miss them.

And then each of them had another thought. What if it's me? What if I'm the Saviour? I'd better take care of myself, do the practices, not gossip so much. I should talk of higher matters if I'm the One, or if I'm not, I might be talking to Them.

Over time, they all started to be more present for their practices and work, and gradually the atmosphere changed. There was a new energy about the place. They had a new reverence for themselves, each other, and Life.

An aura of high consciousness began to radiate from the centre, and people in nearby villages felt it. Word got out, and spiritual seekers began to visit again.

Then some of the young visitors started to talk with the old community members. After a while, one asked if he could join. Then another, and another.

Once again the centre began to thrive. And all thanks to the words of the old holy man.

As this story shows, it only takes one thought to change the world. When you change how you think about yourself, you change everything. If you think of yourself as sacred, you begin to see the sacred in all life. When you see all life as sacred, your own life becomes filled with creative possibility. You awaken the field of unlimited potential.

It's a heyoka story. Many cultures have trickster stories—Loki in the Norse myths, for example, or Sinbad in the "1001 Nights." Among the Indigenous people of the Great Plains of North America, *heyoka* means "sacred clown," the one who flips everything on its head to make us see things afresh. The heyoka breaks the rules, crosses boundaries, disturbs forms. Like the fool at the court of the king, the heyoka is licensed to poke fun. Theirs is the serious business of being outrageous when things get overly solemn, and their role is to set the spirit free.

My grandfather had a big moustache. But he looked so serious you never expected him to joke. One Christmas, he gave me a jack-in-the-box. (I thought it was funny because his name was also Jack.) It was a painted wooden cube, and when you turned the key, it lulled you with gentle music. Suddenly the lid opened, a jolly-jack-joker jumped up, and my sister and I would fall about in giggles. We did it again and again, delighting in the surprise.

Surprise, shock, arouses us. A box is no longer just a box. A wall is no longer a limit. The heyoka smashes open the limits of our mind to think outside the box, see beyond the surface, open to unlimited possibilities. Our spirit wants the freedom to explore new possibilities, and out-of-the-box thinking frees us to access our creative potential.

Thinking "inside the box" doesn't connect us with creativity. Ordinary thought takes our attention away from the present and into the future or past. It sees us as separate and limited in the physical world of form. On the other hand, directing our attention to the present moment opens the door to the infinite potential of the instant. This instant is the portal to extraordinary thought. Ordinary thought is an enemy of awareness, but extraordinary thought is the ally of awakening.

Extraordinary thought breaks us out of the box. It frees our spirit to come out and play. We let go of thinking about the past or future and come into heightened awareness. We connect with the infinite potential of the instant. Inspiration sparks; its sparks catch fire; we feel illuminated with creative possibility. We're ready to make magic.

Einstein is quoted as having said: "No problem can be solved from the same level of consciousness that created it." The challenges we face in our world call us to grow to a new level of consciousness. They call for our magic. They need us to innovate. Innovation comes from inspiration; inspiration from unlimited potential; and unlimited potential from breaking free of our limiting beliefs. There, beyond the edges of what we think we know and who we think we are, we access the field of unlimited potential. We expand to a new consciousness.

Order and organization are essential for the creative, but they need to be fertilized by the unexpected. As some ancient Greeks recognized, creation needs both cosmos and chaos. The heyoka brings chaos, upsetting the existing order and infusing it with fresh life. Creativity is the dynamic dance of these twins, chaos and cosmos.

So what if you are the Saviour? Or are destined to meet them? How will you live your wild and precious life? And how will you shine your luminosity on the world? How will you move to the level of consciousness to which we're called?

PRACTICE: Extraordinary Thought

This practice is intended to deliberately challenge "ordinary" thinking, break you out of the box, and help you access the unlimited potential.

First, think of a situation in which you feel stuck. It could be in a relationship with family or friend, at work, or as part of a creative project. Don't think about this situation in the usual way. Don't think of it as a problem to be solved. Simply bring it into your awareness.

Now put this situation to one side for a moment. If possible, go outside and connect with nature. If this isn't possible, look out of the window or recall a memory of being in nature. Look up at the sky, and take some slow, deep breaths. Breathe fresh oxygen into your blood. The literal meaning of "to inspire" is to breathe in. As you breathe in, imagine fresh inspiration coming into your body and mind. As you breathe out, feel yourself letting go of any preconceived ideas. Notice how your body feels.

After a few deep breaths, you may notice your consciousness has shifted. Now remember a time when you felt free to play with all possibilities. It could be a peak experience, a feeling of connection with the Universe or with the presence of the Divine. Remember how this felt in your body, mind, and spirit. Enjoy this feeling again.

When you have connected with this expansive feeling, look back at the situation. Look at it as if from a high vista or panoramic viewing point. Stay open to possibilities and feel free to experiment and be inventive. If fresh insight doesn't come straight away, be open to it coming to you later. Welcome it when it does.

Let There Be Light

Now that we have opened the field of unlimited potential, let's come into closer relationship with it. What is this light of creation, and how can we become intimate with it?

There are many ways to speak of the "field of unlimited potential": "the void," "quantum field," "spirit," and so on. But to really experience and feel it, we need to let go of labels and concepts.

In essence, it is formless and beyond words. Words are forms that can trap us in mental concepts; we need to find the freedom beyond them. The formless is within forms. The unseen is behind the seen. It is within the sun and stars; they are its visible forms. The space between stars is unseen, but it too is of the light. It too is filled with unlimited potential.

Mystics, madmen, and wise women have spoken of this in many ways. For example, the Persian poet Jalaluddin Rumi wrote:

If ten lamps are in one place, each differs in form from another,
Yet you can't distinguish whose radiance is whose
When you focus on the light.
In the field of spirit there is no division, no individuals exist.[2]

Quantum physicists like Dr. Fred Alan Wolf also speak of light as the essence:

Fundamental particles are made of light, allowing them to disappear, reappear, move forward and backward through time, twisting in space and creating what we perceive as our everyday reality. "Let there be light" takes on a new and profound meaning.[3]

In the vastness of the Universe, the creative light is limitless. Stars are born and grow; they die and transform in supernovae. The fire of these colossal explosions creates new elements. It powers the titan's smithy where they are forged: gold, silver, and iron; oxygen, nitrogen, and carbon; palladium, plutonium, and promethium.

On Earth, these elements combine in many forms—gas, liquid, or solid. But ultimately, they are evolved from light—the light of exploding stars. Before the stars, it is said, light exploded in the Big Bang. It has been expanding and evolving ever since, into stars, minerals, plants, animals, and humans. We are an embodiment of light and part of this evolutionary consciousness.

But creation didn't happen just once, long ago. It is happening all the time. We are in the middle of it, and it is in the middle of us. Our body is made of elements, and we ourselves are expressions of the Universe—we are its children. The field of unlimited potential is within us; the creative is in our every cell.

At conception, each of us starts out as a single cell. From that tiny beginning, we grow ourselves into trillions of cells. This is an amazing feat of creativity, and the essence of the energy we use is light.

Take plants, for example. From algae to orchids and from lichen to lianas, plants transmute the liquid luminosity of sunshine into the elixir of life on Earth. Without the green of their photosynthesis, there would be no food for the animals, and we would not make the red of our blood. Yet all colours are frequencies of the one light. It is ultimately this, the one light, that leaves transmute into food, that pulses through our veins, and that illuminates the galaxy.

How can we awaken our relationship with the one light?

In every person's life there are moments of the extraordinary that expand our sense of Self beyond the ordinary. We transcend limitation and experience a grander vista from which to see our Self and life. During such "peak experiences," feelings of awe and wonder begin to melt into rapture and euphoria. We know our oneness with the Infinite Vastness.

Many things can inspire us to such ecstasy: great art or music, the beauty of a sunset, the birth of new life, or losing ourselves in activity, in frenzied dance, erotic passion, or the exaltation of love. Such moments expand our consciousness, and we touch the timeless beyond time, the formless within form, the unseen beneath the seen. Life blesses us, and its blessing resonates through every cell. We feel the numinous caress of the luminous.

One night when I was a child, my father took me outside and spoke to me about the stars. He pointed out some constellations: the Plough, Orion, and Cassiopeia.

"There's the North Star," he said. "And there, the Seven Sisters."

I remember gazing up in awe as he explained: "They're so far away it takes years for their light to come to us."

Many years later, I again marvelled at the stars. I had gone to the high desert of New Mexico, where my Medicine teachers lived, and was on a vision quest. Vision quest is the practice of being alone and quiet in nature, seeking insight into your life's purpose. I had been fasting and camping on the edge of a canyon for several days and was in a state of acute sensitivity to life.

It was night, and I awoke feeling cold. I stayed in my sleeping bag but wriggled out of the tent. There were no city lights, clouds, or pollution; the sky was spangled with multitudes of stars. Looking up, I beheld their infinite luminosity and felt tears of appreciation. I spoke the words "I love you" to the Universe, and in that moment a star shot from the sky. It silently traced a momentary line of light across the night. It was as if the Universe had said: "Yes, we hear you."

That meteor was a coincidence, yes, but a meaningful one to me. I took it as an affirmation that we aren't separate from creation; we are in relationship with it, and each of us expresses it in our unique way. But creation is extraordinary. We need to open to its mystery for it to inspire us. "Ordinary" thinking closes it off.

I had an earlier peak experience when I was 16. I remember coming home from school one summer evening. It had been another long day.

The sun was shining through the living-room windows, and I sat and bathed my closed eyelids in its light. I focused on the colours I could see through my eyelids: orange, red, and gold. I luxuriated in their lustre and went into a deep state of relaxation. They changed to purple and even green and blue. In this state, I felt no separation, and it replenished me. I only stopped when my mother called me to dinner.

At that time my self-esteem was generally low. I didn't have a loving relationship with myself. I didn't even know there was a Self to be friends with. I felt insecure with my peer group. But that evening when I met some of them at the youth club, I felt immune from their usual teasing. Communing with the light had given me self-confidence: I felt I had the sun's backing. I felt inner resources of which I hadn't been aware. I was in a heightened state of awareness with intense sensitivity to colour. My concentration was enhanced, and that night I played exceptionally well at snooker.

How did that experience come about? Partly from concentration and letting go of ordinary thinking, but also through feeling part of something greater than little me. It taught me that we all have hidden depths and resources. It made me want to know more about psyche and spirit and how to access this richness within.

So now I consider sunbathing a kind of spiritual practice. It is an opportunity not just to relax but to receive the sun's subtle teaching and blessing. Like many of us, I was conditioned to think of the sun as dead matter, but now I hold that it is alive and has consciousness. Sunbathing is communion with the sun's non-human intelligence.

PRACTICE: Golden Woman / Golden Man

I like to do this practice while sitting in the sun, but it can also be done with starlight.

If possible, take off some clothes, and let the sunlight caress your skin directly. Greet the sun and ask it to teach and heal you. Welcome its energy and allow its rays to emanate through your cells. Feel its healing and listen for its subtle teaching.

Breathe slowly and deeply. With each breath, feel the sun's energy replenishing you. Imagine a ray reaching you from the heart of the sun. Direct the energy into your vital energy centres— sex-organs, navel, solar plexus, heart, throat, forehead, brain, and whole body. Breathe the sun into each centre in turn. Let the light clarify your energy field and radiate through your being.

Feel gratitude to the sun. Thank it for giving you life. You may like to see the sun as a man or woman in order to imagine its response. Open to its subtle teaching. Contemplate and commune with the sun. Know that in essence, you are sunlight.

Sunrise and sunset are potent times to take in solar energy. Let yourself go dreamy and let the beauty feed you deeply. Feel your connection with our star, our sun.

A variation of this practice is communing with the stars at night. You can either choose a particular star, a whole galaxy or constellation. Send your blessing and love to the stars and notice what comes back to you. We are not separate from them.

The Magic of Image-Thought

The light of the Universe emanates life force. It is constantly seeking expression. We have the power to shape it by thinking in images. The third step of our journey is to explore this vital faculty of creative consciousness: imagination. All things in the Universe of form have their origin in the formless; everything from stars to stones emerges from the field of unlimited potential. Imagination is our way of touching this divine creativity and affecting its emergence into form. And all things created by humans—including bone tools, the latest software, and this book—began in the formless, in imagination.

Imagine a butterfly. Emerging from egg to caterpillar, it eats voraciously, then hangs upside down, cocooned in chrysalis. During this stage it digests itself, turning into goo, apart from discs of cells that hold the blueprint for wings, antennae, and so on. The discs are aptly named "imaginal" because they awaken a form that wasn't there before—a form of fluttering beauty.

Like the butterfly, we can bring the formless into form. We create sense impressions in the mind without external stimuli. This is imagination, a magical power. Imagination is essential to children's play and development, and it's vital to our growth as adults. It's imagination that suspends our disbelief at the theatre or cinema. It's imagination that conjures up pictures, sounds, and feelings as we read or listen to stories. And it's imagination that transforms consciousness. We need to train ourselves to use it well on our journey.

Here is a story of creativity emerging from imagination.

Rain had confined them indoors for days. Thunder rolled around the mountains, lightning flashed across the lake, and the candles flickered.

It was the wet summer of 1816, and a small party of romantic writers were staying at Lord Byron's villa by Lake Geneva.

That evening, he challenged them each to write a ghost story, and Mary Shelley conceived Frankenstein.

She wrote later that, when she went to bed, "I did not sleep, nor could I be said to think. My imagination, unbidden, possessed and guided me, gifting the successive images that arose in my mind with a vividness . . . I saw the hideous phantasm of a man stretched out; and then on the working of some powerful engine, show signs of life." [4]

Although Mary Shelley describes the imagery as coming to her "unbidden," she had subconsciously invited it. She wanted to respond to Byron's challenge. And they'd had an earlier conversation about whether electricity could bring life or reanimate a corpse. But as she relaxed in bed, imagination gave her the story she told them the next day, the story she published years later, which has gone on to inspire over 50 films.

Imaginative inspiration comes from a different level of the psyche than ordinary thought, but we can call it and be ready to receive it. There are countless stories of creative breakthroughs in many fields that have emerged from waking dreams like the one Mary Shelley received.

But first, let's consider an assumption that can limit our relationship with the Universe: the idea that imagination is not "real." What we consider "reality" in mainstream culture is the material world where the laws of physics apply. That's true, but another way to understand "reality" is to see that it emerges from our states of consciousness. To the brain, everything is symbolic, and what we perceive in the unseen is as real as what we perceive in the seen. Both affect our energy-consciousness.

For a few moments, suspend any doubt over whether imagination is "real," and try this. Imagine your favourite food in detail: its sight, smell, and taste. If you do this vividly enough, there'll be a tangible physiological effect: you'll begin to salivate. Or remember fearing something that later turned out to be harmless. It was "real" at the time because the image generated all the chemicals and physical responses of fear.

Images activate neural networks, causing chemicals to flow in our system. They cause the structure of the brain to change—minutely perhaps, but repetition brings a cumulative effect. In other words, they affect our consciousness and reality. Global industries such as advertising and pornography depend on image-thought to affect behaviour, usually with the aim of causing money to move in a particular direction.

But it is in the power of every individual to command how imagery shapes them. We have the power to change how images affect us and to choose images that evoke wholeness and vitality.

In my training, I learned to choose images from my inner library for the effect they have on my mind and energy. I started with an image of a person embodying courage, kindness, and wisdom. At first, I needed to take time to relax and visualize this image in detail: how they walk, stand, smile. Then I began to feel these qualities myself and to give attention to how they affected me. With practice, it takes only a split second to trigger this neural pathway.

Over time, I developed images to activate each of the eight intelligences. For example, it is often useful to activate healing and nurturing either for others or for oneself. The images we use are entry points that evoke energy, and we can build on them, making them more vivid in the imagination by adding more detail and senses to them.

Hamlet said he saw his father in his "mind's eye," but did he smell him in his mind's nose, or hear him in his mind's ear? We may think of images as visual, but images come in all senses. Multi-sensory images have more evocative power.

There are times when we need to rein in the wild horses of imagination. For example, what happens if you're a parent expecting your child to meet you at a particular time and place, and they don't turn up? It can be easy to go into the fear of "What if?" This can trigger cascades of anxiety chemicals to flood your system. In that circumstance, it's better to contain the imagination. We can then estimate possibilities clearly and decide whether to take action.

And when it comes to imagining the transformation of human consciousness, think of yourself as one of the imaginal cells in the body of the collective consciousness dreaming our common future. "Imagine all the people living life in peace," as John Lennon sang. What will it be like? What will be the new ways of our caring for human needs in harmony with the planet and the needs of plants and animals? Dreaming the future with the power of imagination, these pictures become possible. We draw them to us with the power of consciousness.

PRACTICE: Training Your Inner Senses

This practice trains your imagination by evoking images in each of your inner senses. It also develops your concentration and enhances the vividness of your outer sense-perceptions.

Create a quiet space in which to concentrate. Take four deep breaths and relax. Notice the aliveness in your body and the contact of your body with your seat. Now focus on your inner senses.

Start by evoking a landscape. This can be a place you have been, somewhere you've seen in pictures, or a landscape of the imagination. Evoke it in detail in each sense in turn. For example, imagine a beach: the sound of waves breaking on the shore, the feel of sand underfoot and the touch of breeze on your face, the briny smell of the sea, and the sun rising over the eastern horizon.

Now choose an object to imagine. Experience it with each inner sense in turn. For example, imagine an orange: first, the visual—its shape, pattern, and so on. Then imagine how it feels in your hand—its texture, weight, temperature. Now imagine peeling it and smelling its aroma, and then its taste in your mouth as you take a piece and begin to eat it. Make this as vivid as you can.

Practise imagining other objects, such as aromatic plants like sage, lavender, or roses; sounds such as church bells, violins, or someone calling your name; the texture of various materials; stroking a cat or touching a tree; the taste of chocolate, smell of fresh bread, warmth of sunshine, full moon rising, summer rain falling. Take time to savour each one.

As you return to this practice, you can extend the time you concentrate on each sense to a minute or longer. Training the imagination in this way develops our creativity and is a step on our journey to the centre. We can use it to grow in all areas of our consciousness, as we will see on this unfolding journey.

The Way of Ceremony

 I lacked confidence as a teenager. Deep down I judged myself as not good enough and was ashamed to be me. I wanted friends but didn't know how to be one, certainly not to myself. Often my only companion was loneliness. I hid to avoid the pain caused by these feelings and filled my life with busyness and distraction.

There are many steps a person can take on the path out of loneliness and into relationship. For me, the journey has been marked by ceremony, because ceremony enables us to touch the field of all potential. It provides a form in which we can be informed by the formless and deepen our intimacy with Self, life, and others. And many ceremonies later, I see that the ghost of loneliness no longer haunts me.

When I arrived at my first Medicine ceremony, Leo greeted me with a grin, beard, and silver hair. We'd spoken on the phone, and he'd lured me in, partly with the possibility that I might one day get a job teaching Medicine Wheels. Now he was showing me the way to the group room.

As my hand hesitated on the door handle, I heard laughter from the other side of the door. I stepped into a darkened room filled with a suspicious aroma. There was a group of people sitting on the floor passing round what looked like a large green cigar. But I noticed they didn't inhale. Instead, they were fanning its smoke around them with feathers. Somebody told me later that this was "smudging," a ritual way of cleansing your energy in the aromatic smoke of sage and cedar. Some Native peoples of the Americas do this in preparation for ceremony, respectfully asking the spirits of these plants for blessing. I was shown to a place in the circle. The centre was decorated with candles, crystals, and feathers. In contrast to the long hair and casual clothes of the others, I was wearing grey trousers, a jacket, and tie. I was expecting to join a course, a seminar with notes and lectures, not some kind of party. I'd been to ceremonies before—at church, school, and with the scouts—but I didn't know the rules of this one. Its informality perplexed me, and, worst of all, people seemed to be having fun.

Then Leo began to drum and led us in a song that came from the Mayans:

Ancient Mother, I hear you calling,
Ancient Mother I hear your sound,
Ancient Mother I hear your laughter, Ancient Mother,
I taste your tears.

As we sang, I began to feel more at ease, even though the words were new. It brought us together and raised our energy. But it was the first time I'd sung to a mysterious mother or thought the Divine could be feminine.

Creation, I realize now, is both feminine and masculine. The creative needs these twin principles—one receptive and yielding, the other penetrative and changing. You can see these twins in flowers, animals, and humans. The feminine is being, all potential, the void; the masculine is becoming, activating, movement. The masculine is like lightning that flashes in the darkness of night; it illuminates what is already there in potential. We all have both principles within us.

Regardless of our physical gender, we are both feminine and masculine. Both women and men are able to generate the seeds of fresh inspiration as well as to conceive, gestate, and give birth to new creations. For a long time, the twin principles have been out of balance in mainstream culture; our collective healing begins as we balance them in our Self. A ceremony helps us do so and honour the Creatress Mother and Creator Father in all things.

But in that first ceremony, I was fresh to such ideas. I was new to the idea of the sacred feminine, new to sitting in a circle, and new to this culture. Through all my years at school, I'd been conditioned to think of learning as a serious matter. I'd forgotten that as children we learn a lot through play—play is a serious thing for us in childhood. I didn't know that we adults can continue learning through play, and I thought of ceremony as a serious thing. It is serious, but that does not mean solemn. I was receiving the message that I was allowed to have fun. Indeed, I was allowed to be true to myself.

I didn't know the rules of this ceremony and was nervous about breaking them, whatever they were. The rules are part of the form, and in a Medicine culture there are protocols agreed between people to express respect for each other and life. What is respect? To respect is to look deeply at the Self and others and see beneath the surface. When we respect the Self and others, we open the way to the centre.

We passed a talking stick around the circle. As each person held the stick, they spoke about how they felt, their life challenges, and intention. I'm not sure I revealed very much, but then I hadn't revealed that much to myself. I used to hide because I feared being judged. But people were listening without judgement, and as all our voices were heard, together with the truth of our hearts, it created respect, vitality, and power. It wove our strands together.

I've since been in many ceremonies, some of them baroque and ornate, others Zen-like in simplicity. In essence, a ceremony is a container of energy. We create it with our thoughts, words, and actions, and it enables us to touch and be touched by life. But we can trap ourselves in the form if we cling too rigidly to its sanctity. The form needs to be flexible or it will leak energy. A ritual turns into a rigmarole if we just repeat words or actions without giving them energy. What matters most is the consciousness with which you hold a ceremony. It's not so much *what* you do as *how* you do it.

When you have a thought or feeling it affects the field of energy in and around you. So when people listen to each other in an open-hearted way, they create an atmosphere that helps each person thrive. A ceremony is a field of consciousness we construct not only with the skill of our hands but with the poetry of our words and the beauty in our thought. By creating a container, we make ourselves receptive to the formless, the field of unlimited potential. We connect with the depths and heights of consciousness. In other words, ceremony gives us vertical alignment with the above and below. The horizontal is our daily living in the world; the vertical is our connection with the Universe. It's easy for us to forget this vertical alignment and become engrossed in the horizontal, but we need to awaken both axes to bring the fullness of consciousness into our daily life.

All of life can be a ceremony if we approach it with extraordinary thought. You can make a ceremony of making tea or making love, starting the car or meeting in the boardroom, as long as you are mindful and honouring of your Self and life. Presence is the key, as we'll explore in the next chapter.

That first ceremony gave me a sense of coming home. I felt I had been seen and welcomed in my uniqueness. It made me thirsty to know myself better and become intimate with the Mystery of life. It began to awaken reverence for the Creatress Mother and Creator Father in all things.

PRACTICE: Intimacy with the Universe

The aim of this practice is to reawaken your relationship with the Universe. It can be done alone or in a group. Two powerful times for this are early in the day and late at night.

Perform a ritual action to indicate that you are crossing into ceremony; for example, by washing your hands or lighting a candle. Whatever your ritual action, do it intentionally and mindfully, with reverence for the Mystery and for the spirit of the water and fire.

You can create a container for ceremony by calling in the energies of life: the Great Mystery or Creatress Mother and Creator Father, sun and stars, Earth and planets, water and plants, air and animals. When you "call in" these energies, you evoke your conscious relationship with them.

If you're with a group of people, pass a talking stick and listen to each person as they speak of how they are—emotionally, physically, mentally, and spiritually. If you're alone, take a moment to feel your depths and notice your present condition.

Feel the life force within your body. Notice your breathing. Notice the feeling of vitality within and allow it to move you. Allow your body to dance, without thinking about it. Dance your own unique relationship with the Universe. Be free.

You may then like to do a spiritual practice, such as meditation, prayer, or chanting, or some form of creative expression.

In this way, we reawaken our awareness that we are not separate from life. When that becomes a foundation in our consciousness, everything changes.

Close the ceremony by thanking the spirits that love and care for you, the earth, sun, and life itself. Know that these energies are with you.

The Balance of Being and Becoming

PRESENCE

2

Southeast: Presence

 Our next step is to deepen connection with the Mystery of life through presence. In the East we awakened our relationship with the Universe. This awakening helps heighten our awareness in the Southeast. When we direct attention deeply into the present, we feel spacious and still. Our presence is heightened, and we experience each moment more vividly. We touch the timeless. Our awareness expands to include many levels both in the seen and unseen. We sense the unbroken wholeness of all creation. We are at one with the spirit of life; our presence opens the door to the Great Mystery for us.

The energy centre of the Southeast is the senses: our eyes, ears, nose, mouth, and skin. These are the organs through which we perceive the world. They inform us of what is here now in the present moment. They are the portals through which life touches us and we touch life. This touching only takes place in the present moment, so directing attention to our senses is a way into presence.

It is helpful to distinguish between sensing and thinking. As we'll see, sensing is not the same as labelling or interpreting our sense perceptions. When we direct attention to our sense perceptions we begin to sense stillness. We don't think about stillness; it's the stillness in us that senses stillness in the world. This opens up a lot of inner space to access deep levels of consciousness.

A key to presence is quietening the thinking mind. Noticing stillness gradually brings stillness to the mind. When we do this, we become more aware of our relationship with life and are able to appreciate the beauty within and around us. We also become less identified with the stream of thoughts and have a deeper sense of Self. And we are able to access the wisdom of the source of life, which is within each of us.

One of the causes of our global crisis is an extractive mindset that comes from an uneasy feeling of not having or being enough. To compensate for this sense of lack we may constantly try to get more, but no amount of consumption can truly fill this hole. The real antidote is to become present in our relationship with the earth and Self.

Presence and stillness open directly on the centre of the Self and are the gateway to other realms of consciousness. So they are a vital aspect of our journey to the centre, and we can train our attention to rest in them.

This chapter begins by exploring our potential to do so by **Savouring the Moment**. Presence brings space; space expands awareness; awareness enables observation. By expanding present-moment awareness we can observe any patterns of thought and behaviour that separate us from life. Observation enables us to heal them, and healing supports us to be more present. **A Wizard is Never Late** is a story from my own journey of healing a pattern through observation.

In the third section, we go still deeper into the present and touch the timeless. **A Brief Mystery of Time** explores presence practices such as meditation. This enables us to experience the ever-present eternity of the here and now.

We live in the timeless present, though our thinking is of linear time. **Make Peace with the Present** expands on this realization and explores its implications for our world. Training our attention to be present through deep listening, or any stillness practice, enables us to come home and make peace with the present, and when we are at peace in the Self, we emanate peace into our world.

Savouring the Moment

Cleaning a modern art gallery can be a hazardous business. You're not employed to decide whether a work is rubbish, but several installations have gone in the trash recently. The puddle in Martin Kippenberger's "When it Starts Dripping from the Ceiling" was mopped up; a bag of paper and cardboard by Gustav Metzger was thrown out; and Damien Hirst's impromptu "Morning after the Party"—a collection of beer bottles, coffee cups, and overflowing ashtrays—was cleared away.

I don't know what happened to the cleaners after these incidents, but I appreciate the challenge posed by the artists. They ask us if the emperor has clothes on. What is art? Can we see it in everyday things? Can we open our perception to look with fresh eyes? Can we experience life directly in the moment, without the conditioning of thought or being influenced by a high price tag in a gallery?

Cleaners hunt dirt. Buyers look for products. But hunter-gatherers search for food. And all of us who breathe today are the descendants of hunter-gatherers. As a hunter-gatherer, you need keen senses to find food. Yes, you've learned to read the tracks and signs, but you need to sense subtle vibrations that reveal the presence of game. This means coming into a state of heightened awareness, of deep stillness and presence. It means entering a realm of consciousness innate in all humans. It means coming into the same space as primordial hunters, the consciousness in which a leopard or wolf hunts: pure perception.

To come into pure perception, people who live by hunting and gathering sharpen their senses. In those cultures, young people train their sense perceptions and learn to move quietly, in harmony with the energy field around them, so as not to warn prey of their approach. This kind of education sensitizes them to the subtleties of energy—to "see" beyond the immediate, to "listen" below the surface, to sense the scents carried on the air.

For several years a friend of mine lived with the Hopi in Arizona. She told me they practised using their senses every day, each sense in turn. This was how they trained their attention and moved into pure perception. She shared this practice with me, calling it Feasting your Senses on the World.

I don't live by hunting and gathering, but I practise pure perception in nature. I experienced it on a meditative walking trip to the north of Finland. Coming out from some trees I saw a reindeer browsing. The reindeer must have felt my gaze touch her because she looked up and spread her hind legs ready to run. Usually reindeer bolt, but she watched me for a while and stayed. I stopped moving—physically and mentally—and stopped looking at her directly. Instead, I spread my attention to include the peripheral vision and whole field; this is a good way of being present and connected with your surroundings. She looked at me, decided I was no threat, and went back to browsing. It thrilled my soul.

Letting your attention take in your peripheral vision supports a deeper state of consciousness than when you're dominated by the ongoing chatter of thought. When your gaze becomes diffuse, your mind becomes more still; you are more present and connected with the environment. You blend with the unbroken fabric of life. This is why the reindeer didn't run.

We no longer need these skills to feed ourselves, and our education system doesn't teach them. Until now, most schools haven't trained us how to heighten our sense awareness. But these skills offer great benefits to our growth, learning, and wellbeing. They bring us into the realm of presence.

Training our presence would benefit the education system. A few years ago, I made presentations at my daughter's school, telling the children stories and guiding them in the practice I learned from my friend. Doing it with a class of eight-year-olds brought them into profound stillness, and afterwards they carried on using the practice as part of the school day. The teacher told me it had made her job easier because the kids had become more teachable.

"When I tell them to listen, now they know how to," she said.

Just as the brain is different from the sense organs, thinking is different from perceiving. The two are connected but distinct faculties of consciousness. Life touches us through the senses; this is perceiving. The brain interprets the perception, labelling and making sense of it; this is thinking.

For example, as your eyes take in the pattern of letters on screen or paper, your brain translates these symbols into words and thought. It is the brain, not the eyes, that recognizes the face of a friend, and it is the brain that tells us if something we see is art or simply a mess that needs to be cleared up.

You can't think your way out of thinking, but you can direct your attention onto the sense perceptions. This is a way to deepen your presence and connect with the Mystery of Life. By training your attention to rest on sense perceptions, you gradually quieten your thinking; your brain becomes less restless.

Cultivate an attitude of feasting your senses on the world. Revel in the aromas of shops in the high street: the bakery, stationer's, or coffee house; listen for music in the whispers of the wind, voices in the river, or poetry of the birds; marvel at the masterpieces of sunset or cloudscape, or the patterns of light dancing on ocean waves. Delight also in the tactility of texture as you meet matter on the shores between Self and other.

Feasting your senses on the world trains your perception. It opens the door to presence, and through that portal is the Deep Self. Right now is the moment of power, the only moment. All past and future are contained within it. Savouring this moment through the senses brings vitality. It awakens us to the preciousness of life.

Right now, I look up from writing to see my dog sitting on the lawn. She is simply listening to the wind in the trees. Like most animals, she's a maestro of presence.

I also notice the clutter of cups and plates around me. Having touched the timeless, I realize the time; my wife will be home soon. Could I tell her it's an art installation and potentially valuable? Should I choose to call it "Tidy Kitchen" or "Mess Is in the Eye of the Beholder"? Whatever I do about the state of the kitchen, I choose to be present with my senses and the beauty of each moment.

PRACTICE: Feast Your Senses on the World

This is a practice in directing attention to the sense perceptions. The key is to let go of thoughts about the perceptions.

Notice your whole field of vision, including the periphery—above, below, and to the sides. Usually, we're only aware of where our eyes are pointing. Shifting attention to the peripheral vision is a powerful way to access stillness and deepen consciousness. As you open the whole field of vision, allow the world to come to you— colours, shapes, movement, light, and dark.

You can use it in the middle of activity; for example, driving, walking, or in a meeting.

Spend five minutes on each of your senses in turn: five minutes listening as sound caresses the ear; five minutes focused on touch; five minutes receiving scents; five minutes tasting a mouthful of food.

When you listen, open yourself to the Universe of sound. Allow the sensations of sound to come in without labelling them; just attend to the quality of sound in each moment.

Then attend to the touch of your clothes, skin, or things around you. Give full attention to the tactile sense for five minutes; observe the various textures.

You can practise smell by bringing things with a strong smell to your nose, such as herbs, flowers, or incense. Or you can put your nose close to things. In this way, you can detect the odour of such common things as stones, leaves, and earth.

Tasting is not the same as "eating." It means taking in a mouthful and noticing the sensations in your mouth. Notice if they change as you direct attention to them.

When you practise this in nature, notice the presence of the beings of nature, such as trees, water, or the weather. Their presence draws us into presence. Gradually, you realize that presence is everywhere, and sensing it heightens awareness in each moment.

You can of course practise feasting your eyes on the world during everyday activities. Notice, for example, the texture, weight, and temperature of things you often touch — door handles, computer mouse and keyboard, or the car steering wheel. Direct your attention as you bring food from your plate to your mouth, and then to its taste and texture. Or give yourself the gift of pausing to listen to music or whatever sounds are occurring. These are ways to turn regular activities into mini-meditations for awakening.

Practices like this, "Training your Inner Senses" (p. 40) and other stillness practices enhance our perceptual sensitivity.

A Wizard Is Never Late

 Our next theme is the power of observation. Stillness and presence give us inner space in which to observe ourselves, and observation gives us access to the deep waters of the Self. Cultivating these qualities is vital for our onward journey of consciousness.

"A wizard is never late,"[5] says Gandalf in the movie of Tolkien's *The Lord of the Rings*. "He arrives precisely when he means to." It reminds me of something my teachers told me: "Medicine people are never in a hurry. Sometimes they move fast, but they don't rush."

I couldn't imagine what my teachers meant. It was an exotic thought, the idea of being neither late nor in a hurry; I was usually both. But their words made me curious, and I decided to observe this pattern more closely.

I began to notice that I was always pushing to get places quicker or get things done as soon as I'd started them. I had two guests in my mind— Hurry and Worry—whispering thoughts like *I haven't got time*. I'd be chuntering along like the White Rabbit in Alice in Wonderland: "Oh, dear! Oh, dear! I shall be too late! Oh, my fur and whiskers."[6] I realized that things were bad when I noticed the irony of rushing to a relaxation class. Actually, I was causing a lot of stress on my mind and body.

Another time, I found that I was running early for an appointment, so I decided to stop off at a shop to buy bread and butter. I thought it would save time later, although we had other food in the house. Inside the shop there was a queue, and I began to get impatient; my blood pressure rose rapidly. Back on the road, the traffic in front was moving as if for a funeral, and by the time I reached my appointment I wasn't simply late, I'd boiled over with stress. I could see that this level of stress would eventually kill me, so I asked my teacher what to do to transform this pattern. "Get present," he emphasized. "You need to stalk this pattern and see what's behind it. Get present so you've got enough awareness, then you can make a strategy how to heal."

After this I gave the pattern a name—Hurry-Worry—and began setting my intention every morning to observe it. In the evening I'd record what I'd learned in my daily log. I realized that I had little relationship with flow or timing. Gradually, I surfaced the thought-phrases that triggered Hurry-Worry, thoughts like *Quick, come on, Out of my way*, or *I'm going to be late*. I started to become conscious of the attitudes and beliefs behind this pattern.

Behaviours are like plants growing in the garden of consciousness. If you want to change, you need to do inner gardening; you need to see what's growing in your garden. The beliefs behind a pattern are the root structures, partially buried in the soil of your subconscious. Awareness is your spade: you use it to dig the plant up. Then you can see the roots and soil clinging to them. How was this pattern planted? What thoughts have helped it grow? With awareness you begin to change the pattern. But not only do you need to remove the "weed," you also need to plant a different pattern, because Nature abhors a vacuum.

One of the roots of this "weed," Hurry-Worry, was the idea that time was a commodity. I'd often heard my father say "Time is money" or my teachers at school telling me not to "waste time," and I had a general feeling of not enough time. I'd come to believe that waiting was a waste of time, so I'd fill every possible minute with busyness before setting out.

Another root was my fear of being late. At school, we'd be judged and punished for lack of punctuality. Being late was tantamount to being a "bad" person.

Coming to understand the underlying beliefs enabled me to lovingly re-educate myself. I consciously chose new thoughts such as *I have all the time in the world* or *Everything that really needs to get done today will get done*. Gradually these changed my patterns of energy and behaviour.

I also interviewed Hurry-Worry to understand it better. I did this in the sanctuary of my bath, wallowing in warm water and bubbles and talking to the taps as if they represented this pattern. I discovered that Hurry-Worry was "only trying to help." I asked him what I needed in order to heal. His answer was so simple it surprised me: "Why don't you set out earlier?"

Most important was learning to accept the present moment as it is. I developed a new attitude to waiting. Instead of seeing it as a waste of time, I could simply enjoy the present. This enabled me to look ahead and estimate timing.

Working on Hurry-Worry and presence has given me a better awareness of flow. Opposite the Southeast is the Law of Cycles in the Northwest. Energy moves in cycles, some of which are obvious: the pulse of day and night, the waxing and waning of the moon, the cycle of the seasons. Others are less apparent: the sunspot cycle, the precession of equinoxes and yet vaster cycles like the spiralling dance of galaxies. And energy moves in cycles in our human world; the economy has rhythms, and so do conversations and the flow of traffic.

The reason wizards are never late is because they operate from inside the moment. Inside the moment is outside of time. The moment wizards arrive is the present moment, and it's the only moment they could arrive. We can all practise wizardry, and if ever you should need to be a Time Lord and bend the laws of the Universe, the only possible way to do so is outside of time.

Meanwhile, in the collective reality of everyday life, you may still turn up "late" and need to apologize to people you kept "waiting." Babbling some mystical mumbo-jumbo about the timelessness of the present moment won't do.

And boats, buses, and trains don't wait. A couple of years ago we set out for the summer holiday only to find the road to the airport clogged with slow-moving traffic. We missed our flight—something I'd often felt anxious to avoid. But I worked with the challenge of staying present; in the past I'd have wasted energy fretting and emitting pushy vibes towards the cars and caravans in front. We found ourselves on an entirely different adventure from the one we'd imagined. And we caught the teaching to "set out earlier."

Practices for Stillness

WALKING MEDITATION. Walk in silence. Focus on your feet touching the ground, and keep the same rhythm of walking. Imagine each footstep caressing the earth with prayer. If thoughts occur, notice them and let them go. Bring your attention back to your feet. Be present in each moment without thinking about getting to a destination.

SLOW MOVEMENT. Move slowly, giving attention to how your body feels as you move. Also include everything around you in your attention. Open your whole field of vision to include the periphery. You could take as long as a minute to take one step, but keep moving forward, even if almost imperceptibly. You can use this walk to come close to animals because they will be less startled by your movement.

THIRTY-SECOND HOLIDAY. Give yourself a 30-second holiday using your sense-perceptions. Look around your current location. Notice your surroundings: the ceiling, walls, and furnishings if you're inside; the land and sky if you're out. Notice things that you don't ordinarily give attention to, such as shadows, reflections, and spaces between objects. This creates a space of presence and centres you. It's especially helpful if you're feeling stressed.

BREATH AWARENESS. Let your attention rest on the air flowing in and out of your lungs. When thoughts arise let them go, and return your attention to the breath. Use breath as the object for meditation, letting your attention be with its movement at the nostrils, abdomen, or anywhere in your body.

A Brief Mystery of Time

Time is a mystery. It stretches to infinity. The past is gone; the future is yet to be; and we exist here, on this fleeting sandbank of the present. Time is fleeting, and yet this very moment is part of the continuum of all moments. It is connected with all time. It lasts forever.

But how long is the present moment? Shorter than a day, an hour, a minute, the present doesn't even last a second. A "jiffy" is the shortest unit of time so far invented—it's faster than the speed of thought—but the present doesn't even last that long.

Does time take any time at all? Does it pass at the same speed for everyone? Do ants, aardvarks, or zebra fish experience it the same as humans? Or does the speed of time vary according to your state of consciousness?

No, what we call "time" is simply a collective agreement. It's convenient for meetings and the effective functioning of civilization. That's why we created devices called "clocks," which undergo movement and change at a regular rate. By convention, we align these devices with the rhythm of Earth's dance around the sun, and divide each rotation into 24 hours. We interpret the changes in these devices to tell where we are in the dance of day and night and decide whether we're "late" or not. They help us coordinate our complex activities and meet each other without having to wait days. But clocks tell us nothing about consciousness or the mystery of the ever-present moment.

There are meditation practices in which you focus on your breathing. You direct your attention to the breath and align with a different rhythm, an internal one. Every so often you notice the occurrence of thinking, then you let go of thinking and direct your attention back to the breath. You choose to be present and not think about the past or future or of getting anything. Being with the flow of inhale and exhale, your breath slows down, you drop into deeper consciousness, and your sense of time changes.

In practices such as this, you step out of time and into the "timeless." The timeless is always present, but we're often not aware of it because we're focused on getting somewhere or something. When we're busy we're often caught up in time and forget about the timeless. It's helpful to make spaces in time to be in the timeless, because we can learn to operate in the world of time from within the timeless.

The first time I tried meditation, I'd been reading a book about yoga that suggested putting your attention on a candle flame for five minutes. I was shocked that it was so difficult: I couldn't last five seconds without thinking.

Some years later I made friends with Roger. Until recently he'd been a Buddhist monk. He invited me to a meditation session with such enthusiasm that I agreed: "Come on," he said. "It's a roomful of people just being with their breath. Just for an hour. Surely you can spare an hour?"

That hour lasted for eternity. I was so bored. Nothing happened. Nobody said anything. Everyone sat cross-legged with eyes closed. I sat still. I shuffled around. How long could an hour last? I shuffled again. The clock didn't move. Nobody spoke. Nothing happened . . . again. And finally, relief, someone sounded a bell, and I found I'd survived the ordeal.

In spite of that part of me that thought that I was bored, I went back to Roger's meditation group and started practising regularly. Gradually, I stopped trying to think my way out of thinking because repeated attempts showed this to be futile. And I gave up labelling that state of consciousness "boredom." Instead, I connected with a deeper part of myself, a more ancient or timeless part. I began to feel at home there, connected with all time.

There is a crack between the worlds, a gap between "tick" and "tock." When you slip into that gap you merge with the timeless. You're so absorbed that time flies. This moment is eternal, ever present. As poet William Blake said, you "Hold Infinity in the palm of your hand And Eternity in an hour."[7] And yet trying to hold onto this moment is like trying to grab a piece of soap you've dropped in the bath. The tighter you grab, the further it shoots away. Better to let go of the struggle; better to be present with effortless effort.

When you meditate, don't try to meditate. Let go of the past and future and allow a gap between thoughts. Be alert in the stillness, the silence without thought. If thinking happens, notice it and let it go. Simply be with the silent vastness of the moment. Don't try to get anything out of it: there is nothing to get. No struggle, no problem, simply being; all is well.

Being present is easy. If only the present exists, where else could we be? This moment is the only moment; we cannot be in any other moment. We say things like "the mind wanders," but where can the mind wander to? There's nowhere for the mind to go. The attention meanders into plans or memories or other distractions that seem more interesting than the object of meditation, but it can only meander in the present moment.

Busyness of thought separates us from experiencing our oneness with all life. We can't connect with oneness or touch the timeless through thinking, because the thinking part of us cannot imagine not thinking; it only knows thinking. And thinking can be such a habit that we might think that all we are is thinking, or that "consciousness" is the same as thinking. But consciousness is infinitely vaster. We live in the timeless as well as within time. We experience ourselves in the passage of time because we have memory and the ability to imagine the future. But continuously thinking about past and future separates us from the infinite ever-present. Here, in this moment, is our limitless potential. Here, in the now, is our greatness.

Past, present, and future are properties of consciousness. Memory of the past and planning for the future take place within the present. The fourth element is movement or change, because everything on the wheel of time moves and changes. Movement and change are in the direction of energy, the Northeast. These four are in the non-cardinal directions: present in the Southeast, past in the Southwest, future in the Northwest, and movement and change in the Northeast. But we need to be present to access the other realms of consciousness as our journey unfolds.

We can imagine time and the timeless as a cross. The horizontal axis is the everyday world of time—of alarm clocks, appointments, and diaries. The vertical is the timeless. Letting go of thought makes spaces in time. When we make spaces in time, we remember the vertical dimension. When we touch the timeless, we touch the Infinite in who we are. In a mysterious way this is the Essence–Self, the centre of our circle.

PRACTICE: Touching the Timeless

This form of meditation deepens awareness of the ground in which thought occurs.

Start by taking several deep breaths consciously. Then focus on the in-breath and out-breath as your object of meditation. Listen to your internal dialogue consciously.

Observe your thoughts as they arise, but also notice the "gap" between them. Thoughts want to catch your attention and carry it away. Give them your blessing, let them pass, and return your attention to the gap between them.

Giving attention to anything brings energy to it. As you give attention to the gap of stillness beyond thought, stillness grows. Your thinking gradually becomes more still, and you come into a state of peace consciousness. Here there is no stress or strife. You touch the timeless and rest in primordial oneness.

Observe the urge to fill your consciousness with thought. For example, when you're waiting, you may feel the urge to reach for a thought-generator, such as a phone, book, or screen. But observing this tendency and choosing to practise stillness gives you the option to fill consciousness with presence.

Your awareness expands to include deeper levels of consciousness. You can practise this awakening of consciousness anywhere.

Make Peace with the Present

Presence is a door to "being," and being is the complement of "doing." As human beings, our attention is often filled with doing, but if we forget to be beings and only do doings, we become unbalanced. But when doing emerges from being there's no stress—only inner stillness and outer movement.

A simple practice that opens the door is deep listening. You listen deeply just by noticing what you hear. You notice both the sounds and the silence behind them. You notice thoughts as if they were bubbles rising to the surface of a pond, and you're aware of the water in which they rise. You notice your present situation, and you notice your needs and wants as they call for attention.

Deep listening goes beyond ears, behind appearance, and beneath the surface. Senses open, heart open, mind open, we allow the present moment to flow through us with beauty and mystery. We receive it without getting caught up in the stream of thinking. Receiving with openness and presence, heart and spirit, body and feeling, deep listening enables us to notice nuance and subtlety, to be with the essence behind things, thoughts and words. It rests our attention in the timeless Self.

There's nothing "wrong" with shallow listening. It simply means that part of our attention is on something else. We may be directing it there, or perhaps it's been captured and stolen away by that thief of presence, thought, or sucked into a thought-generator, such as a screen or book. But shallow listening can cause stress if we're disconnected from being or resisting the present moment. This blocks our connection with the centre of the Self. I have an image of deep listening in Agustín, someone I met on a journey in the great rainforest of Amazonia. He wore a cap, T-shirt, shorts, and flip-flops. His skin was the deep brown of old leather and etched like a map with all the trails he'd followed through the forest. I sat behind him in a dugout canoe, paddling until my arms ached, watching him steadily stroke the water through this endless wilderness.

We paddled to the bank and walked into the forest. We came to an area where palm fronds had fallen like fans, and he signalled me to stop. I sensed his stillness, his awareness intense, listening profound, and followed him into this state of consciousness.

I was one with the forest. There was no separation. Its symphony of pulsing insects was me; no thought needed to ripple across the surface of my mind. It was then that we saw a capybara and its young. They ran across the glade, and joy surged in my heart.

Living within nature had taught Agustín to be at home in silence. Silence didn't threaten him. He didn't need to fill outer space with words or inner space with thought. He was able to rest in being, in communion with life, where there's no separation between the listener and the listened and no clear distinction between subject and object, inner and outer. He moved through the forest in silent knowing.

As a domesticated European, I'm familiar with the habit of inner chatter. I know the awkwardness that silence can produce. My teacher spoke of "the silence that drives the white man mad," meaning the silence with which Native elders met the questions asked by European settlers in the Americas. But I also know that there's something Indigenous in our soul, even if it's buried beneath layers of conditioning. Everyone has the potential for silent knowing.

When Indigenous elders sit in council, their aim is to surface the collective wisdom to make wholesome decisions, and their way is deep and respectful listening. This allows different perspectives to be heard and honoured. It allows disagreements to surface in order to process them rather than risking their escalation into division and war. This old way of politics would serve us well now, but it requires effort to resolve polarities instead of settling them with majority votes. The advantage is that it leads to growth and greater understanding. Wholeness emerges.

You can be open or closed to another person's words. You can listen with the attitude of wanting to understand their feelings, concerns, and where they're coming from. Or you can listen with *Yes, but* . . . in your mind, looking for ways to prove them wrong. Unsatisfactory communication is widespread in our world.

I remember an argument with my wife. We've had many arguments before and since; disagreements are inevitable in close relationships between equals, and both of us are fiery. I don't recall what we disagreed about, but I remember the energy and how it moved.

That morning I'd been diligent with my practices. I'd gone outside, felt the air, and greeted the sun. I'd awoken to the Infinite with the power-thought *I am in your Universe; your Universe is in my body; your Universe and I combine together.* I'd sat for a while listening to the wind and birdsong, and had reached out with my attention to the plants, planet, and Self. I'd also practised emanating love to the landscape and to particular people. At the end of my morning practice, I'd returned inside, had breakfast, and begun the activities of the day.

A few hours later we were discussing something in the kitchen. We'd both been triggered and were reacting to each other in attack and defence. We were exchanging words in salvos. The stress was escalating. Part of me wanted to withdraw, and I noticed I'd backed up against the cooker. My wife was the other side of the table. The blood was up, the tension high, and neither of us was prepared to lose.

Usually when emotional stress rises, awareness falls. For a while, this was no different, except that I had a sudden eruption of awareness. Instead of staying stuck on the same track of thinking how best to argue back, I had a different kind of thought: *I love her.* I felt it and looked at her in a different way. I suddenly saw her anew, not just as an enemy shouting at me. The whole shift took place on the inside, and it was a miracle. A spell broke. The clamour stopped, the trumpets muted, the guns silenced. Neither of us gave up; we just stopped fighting.

Having awoken this state of stillness in the morning, it was easier to access it later in the heat of conflict. My morning practice had enabled me to carry stillness with me into the day. Deep listening gives us presence, spaciousness, and awareness. It supports our emotional intelligence, the subject of the next chapter. My wife and I are learning to be more present in our councils. We're able to be open, especially when there is disagreement or a surge of emotional energy. When my inner voices begin to clamour to speak, my practice is to give myself the command, *Receive!* Receptivity opens the space inside to truly listen. True listening heightens awareness, and heightened awareness brings us into deeper connection with the Self, life, and others.

Receptive, spacious, and connected—these are qualities that emerge through presence; serene, understanding, and appreciative—these are gifts we generate when we make peace with the moment. When we are awake to our oneness with the Universe and the Infinite Ever-Present, then we are able to carry these energies forward to the next direction of the wheel.

PRACTICE: Deep Listening

Practise deep listening in nature. Sit with a landscape, seascape, or night sky. Open your ears, eyes, and skin to receive. Allow sounds to come into you without labelling or thinking about them. Release any verbal thoughts about the sounds. Let your mind be still. Listen intently.

Saint Ignatius Loyola spoke of listening so intently that you could hear the sound of the stars. Let your awareness expand and open wide. Listen to the Universe—not only to sounds but to silence, not only to stars but to space.

Listen to the Infinite Vastness within and all around.

Practise deep listening to another person. Listen not only to their words and expressions, but to their inner being, the formless Self behind their speech. Have no judgement. Let go of formulating your responses or putting your opinion forward.

Giving them your attention like this builds understanding and intimacy.

Practise deep listening to yourself. Listen to your breath. Make space for your feelings and listen to any voices that have not been heard. Notice your thoughts, feelings, and memories as they arise, but also notice the background consciousness in which they occur. Listen for deeper insight and for the wisdom that is within you. Listen to your body. Notice any physical sensations and the vital life force within.

Deep listening heightens awareness. Listen to the sacred music of the birds, wind, and river. They speak not in the tongues of men but in the ten thousand voices of spirit. Their song is one song: the Universe. Let it resonate through your being and restore your unbroken wholeness.

Opening the Door to Great Mystery

3

South: Emotion

On the East, we awakened our oneness with creation. In the Southeast, we deepened through presence and awareness. Our next step is to build on these energies and harness the power of emotion for our growth. This will also enable us to process and resolve many of the conflicts in our world.

The element in the South of the Medicine Wheel is water. This is also the direction of plants, the sacred green world of growth: grass and grain, fruit and flowers, herbs, trees, and cacti. Plants are the first-born of earth and sun. Living in the ground and consuming light, plants have the marvellous ability to transform rays of sunlight into growth. Without this power of plants we humans could not live, and we owe them our gratitude and respect.

As I look out of the window from where I'm writing, I see a plant growing high up on the building opposite. It's clinging tenaciously to a crack that's only just big enough to gather water. Swaying in the breeze, it has an indomitable urge to live and grow. It reminds me that some plants even crack their way through pavement, so powerful is their yearning for the light.

The essence of the South is the power of growth. This is in humans as well as plants. We call it emotion, and in some ways, it's like water. Both water and emotion take many forms. Emotion ebbs and flows like the tides. It can be calm like a lake, stagnant like a pool, or flowing like a mountain stream. It can freeze like ice or rage like a storm at sea. And like water, emotion is always in us, whether we're aware of it or not.

Human emotions are complex. They can bring us into conflict or drive us into actions we later regret. Or we can suppress them and constrict our growth. Some emotions are easier than others, but in essence, emotions are neither good nor bad, neither positive nor negative; they are simply life energy moving within us. There's no need to judge ourselves or others for having them; emotions enable us to experience the full spectrum of being human.

Can we respond to feelings, or do they drive us into reaction? Anger, for example, is a natural feeling that alerts us when something's out of balance or a boundary has been crossed. But can we express it in ways that lead to greater wholeness? Are we present enough to hear what our feelings are telling us without getting caught by them? And are we able to learn from them and deepen the wisdom of our heart?

An aspect of emotional power is our openness to experience, because experience brings growth. We embark on this voyage of discovery in this chapter with **The Little Child of the Universe**, which explores openness, trust, and innocence. These qualities enable us to use emotional power for our growth.

All of us have painful emotional experiences. We want to avoid distress, but avoidance makes pain linger. It can take a lifetime to heal ourselves, learn to manage our feelings, and open to beauty. We may then see our painful experiences as simply the blows that have tempered us on Life's anvil. Emotion can lead us to war; peace calls for our discipline. **Wholeness in Diversity** is about the discipline needed to let this power of growth take us into our heart-wisdom.

Truth and Reconciliation is about the power of vulnerability and tough love. These qualities are needed for us to reestablish peace and wholeness.

React or Respond shows how presence supports this power of growth to bring wholeness in the moment and enables emotion to fuel our journey to the centre.

The Little Child
of the Universe

The power of emotion moves us to learn through experience. When we're little children, we learn rapidly, thanks to our freshness and curiosity. We are trusting, innocent, and open to the adventure of life. We feel deeply without getting stuck in feeling.

Like most children, I was fascinated by many things when I was little—earthworms wriggling in my hand, clouds gliding across the window, the smell of the sea. I remember dancing with dust motes in the golden glow of a sunbeam, marvelling at the blackness of soot from inside the chimney, and listening to the language of birds. I half-understood their messages. Animals were all around: a cuddly bear, chimp, and elephant shared my bed, and lions, giraffes, and rhinos were all over the wallpaper. I knew I was related to animals and to the whole Universe.

My dad told me to grow up, so I did. And as I did, I learned to see myself more and more as a separate, competing ego. I came to identify with "my" stuff, "my" experiences, and "my" opinions. I hid my sensitivity, shut down curiosity, and anaesthetized awe and wonder.

But I've learned that the qualities we have as little children remain inside us our whole life—at least, in potential—despite the warps and wounds of time and cares and concerns of adulthood. Whatever our physical age, we have childlike qualities. "Childlike" doesn't mean "childish;" it means "fresh, open, and trusting, able to feel awe and wonder at life, keen to explore, discover, and learn through experience." These qualities turn on the vital juice of our life force.

There is a little child with these energies inside us. It is an expression of our emotional mind. As with plants, this part of us has the power of growth, and it is emotional energy that propels growth. This power is obvious in little children. They are sensitive to deep feeling, but they are also examples of fluidity, because their emotions flow without getting stuck. They learn rapidly, but whatever our age, the childlike potential for growth stays with us.

This is not to deny the impact of childhood abuse or the enormous need to heal trauma. This healing is essential for our collective evolution. But recognising our innate sensitivity and innocence—hidden though they may be—is part of the healing.

How can we access this potential? How can we activate awe and wonder in life and trust in Self? How do we use the power of the little child for our growth and wellbeing?

Kid's stories are full of animals, like Winnie the Pooh:

"Rabbit's clever," said Pooh thoughtfully.
"Yes," said Piglet. "Rabbit's clever."
"And he has Brain."
"Yes," said Piglet. "Rabbit has Brain."
There was a long silence.
"I suppose," said Pooh, "that that's why he never
understands anything." [8]

I don't completely agree with Pooh about this. All my life I've aspired to being clever, and I believe having brain is good. It enables us to understand many things, such as science, languages, and machines. But the little child doesn't identify with being clever. The trick is not to let the brain-mind close us off to the messages of our emotional-mind or the knowing of our heart. Not knowing makes space in which to learn, space for inspiration, space for life to stroke us with beauty. Be clever but open to learning: this is the beginning of wisdom. As the Zen master Shunryo Suzuki said:

"In the beginner's mind there are many possibilities, but in the
expert's there are few." [9]

What is Beginner's Mind?

Beginner's Mind is an open mind, empty of opinion, assumption, and prejudgement.

An open mind is able to learn from anyone and anything, anywhere. A beginner focuses on each step, not thinking about getting somewhere else. This open presence heightens awareness and appreciation. Life becomes an adventure of possibility, and you live each moment to the full.

We never really know what's going to happen next. Beginner's Mind is open to the unexpected. It's willing to try things without attachment to the outcome. It's not inhibited by fear of getting it wrong or making a mistake, because a "mistake" is a chance to learn something. With Beginner's Mind we meet life with trust and innocence, letting ourselves experience whatever we experience.

Trust is a journey of learning to be true to one's Self; innocence means letting go of pretence. Trusting the power that flows from within, there's no need to pretend, no need for hiding or camouflage. In our essence we are innocent. We were born innocent, and innocence is our natural state. Guilt is only a sign that there's a lesson for us to learn, a pattern for us to change.

But trust does not mean naivety, and innocence doesn't mean ignorance. They do not mean that we aren't alert to danger, don't assess risk, or use street wisdom; we just don't let external threats rob us of power.

I sometimes work on a project with young people aged around 14 and 15. Many of them lack confidence, and the aim is to help them gain it through a closer relationship with their Self. We guide them into challenges like climbing (with safety harness), kayaking (with lifejacket), and handling birds of prey (with a falconer). These activities are "safe" but outside many of the young people's comfort zones. At first many of them resist taking part, but afterwards they feel thrilled by the victory of having faced their fear and participated. They feel happy with themselves.

When we explore our "edge" with awareness and support, we're in the learning zone. It's here that we awaken a heightened connection with life, Self, and Universe, and that connection builds our trust.

It's good to feed the urge for adventure with new experiences. One time, I took a ship from Greece to Egypt. When I arrived in Alexandria, everything was so vivid! I found myself illiterate again, unable to read the Arabic signs. I was fascinated by the people, clothes, buildings, and streets; struck by the plants, soil, and the warmth of the African breeze; curious about everything; thrilled with discovery; and filled with life energy. Even the food intrigued me, with its faint flavour of desert dust.

Regular adventures feed us, but we don't have to go on major expeditions. We can feel little child energy with a simple thought. As Piglet said to Pooh:

> *"When you wake up in the morning, Pooh," said Piglet at last,*
> *"what's the first thing you say to yourself?"*
> *"What's for breakfast?" said Pooh. "What do you say, Piglet?"*
> *"I say, 'I wonder what's going to happen exciting today?'" said Piglet.*
> *Pooh nodded thoughtfully. "It's the same thing."* [10]

I find that whether I'm in the city or the country, at home or on the road, little child energy infuses life with vim, vigour, and vitality. When I look with new eyes and listen with fresh ears, curiosity turns up in the most unexpected places. Or I ask myself a question like *What haven't I noticed before?* and suddenly I'm engaged with the moment again. Innocence opens the door that lets beauty into the inner sanctum of the Self. We become intimate friends with the Universe again and touch into the cradle state of consciousness.

PRACTICE: Beginner's Mind

This practice supports you to move forward with trust and innocence. It refreshes vitality and enables you to access the emotional power of growth.

Evoke Beginner's Mind with questions like these: "What arouses my sense of adventure? What am I curious about in my Self and life? What new things am I discovering?"

Suspend ordinary thinking, and let go of preconceptions. Imagine what it would be like if you'd just arrived from a galaxy far, far away. Look at things as though you've never seen them before. Notice what you usually filter out of awareness. Deliberately open your senses to newness—fresh eyes, clean ears, new hands.

There has never been a moment like this. Open to it with awe and wonder. Allow life to touch you; let beauty caress your soul. Be sensitive to the vital essence shimmering within you and in everything around you.

In this state, be curious about your feelings. Welcome the currents of emotion, including the subtle feelings beneath the surface.

Sometimes, emotion is left over from the past. With the attitude of Beginner's Mind, you can revisit past feelings and heal them by freeing up stuck energy.

You can also go into Beginner's Mind when approaching a problem. What assumptions have been limiting your response? You may find fresh insight or a novel approach to the challenge.

Wholeness in Diversity

 Life is full of endless diversity, not only in plants and animals but in other humans, too. Sometimes we feel mistrust when we encounter the diversity of strangers. We can tend to identify with "our" group and feel suspicion of the "other." Beginner's Mind enables us to meet difference with trust and openness. This leads to greater wholeness and is the second step of our journey in the realm of emotion.

There were lots of trees at the bottom of the garden where I grew up. We used to play in one tree in particular, a sycamore that forked into two trunks close to the ground. At first, I couldn't climb beyond the fork and used to watch my sister and her friends go higher. They would step across from one trunk to the other—something they called "Making London Bridge." But when I was older, I used to climb to the top and sway in the breeze, playing the lookout in the crow's nest of a ship at sea.

Many years later, I danced in ceremony to a tree at the centre of a circle. It was a cottonwood tree, trimmed so you could see that its trunk went into twin forks, like a "Y." It represented life and the oneness of creation. The oneness of the Universe is expressed through complimentary opposites, such as feminine and masculine or being and becoming. These twin opposites give birth to the "ten thousand things," the vast diversity of life's expressions—stars, planets, plants, animals, and so on.

Back and forth we danced, again and again, from periphery to centre and back again, drawing energy from the Tree of Life. Moving in and out of the centre was a metaphor for the pulse of life, the universal breathing in and breathing out, expansion and contraction. And as we continued to dance between centre and periphery, we began to experience states of consciousness beyond these polarities. Light and dark, day and night are one great holy circle; hot and cold, summer and winter are poles of the yearly cycle, and all things, every one of us, are conceived of masculine and feminine.

Creation is One; all of humanity's wisdom traditions point us towards this. The One is expressed through twinness and the twinness through the ten thousand things of the world.

The purpose of the ceremony was to come into a state of peace. Being at peace brings peace into the world. Peace is not the opposite of war; it is the resolution of polarities through deepening our relationship with the oneness behind them. An epiphany is a realization of unity consciousness, and our intention in the dance was to experience epiphany: to go beyond separation into unity.

There is an ancient teaching of the forked tree that reflects the way we see ourselves in relation to the "other." One fork represents "me;" the other fork the "other," everything we don't identify with. You and I are branches from the same trunk. If I look at you as "bad," I become "bad" myself, because we are One, but if I see you as a reflection of things about myself that I haven't yet seen, I open to the teaching.

When you start fighting against something, it's easy to become like it. Years ago, I had a girlfriend who persuaded me to become involved in the anti-apartheid movement. We often discussed the wickedness of the racist regime, and I noticed inside I started to feel racist towards the white South Africans. But the problem was not the people in their essence; it was the distortion of consciousness, the "us and them" thinking that created apartheid. And judging the "other" drew me into a similar distortion.

Peace doesn't mean we don't stand up for the oppressed, whether the oppressed are other people, species, or parts of the planet. We need to stand up for them, because they are part of us. But so are the oppressors. There is an effective way to challenge oppression that promotes peace because it goes beyond "us and them" thinking. It's the way that Mandela, Tutu, and other South Africans challenged apartheid and changed the system without great bloodshed.

A good way to offer this kind of challenge is by being present and connected with our centre. Our centre is the centre of the Universe, the source of universal love. When we communicate from this consciousness, we help the "other" find their way back to their centre. It's as if activating the centre in us activates it in the "other." Being conscious of the oneness behind diversity creates a field of consciousness, and that field may awaken in the ones we're challenging.

We go beyond "us and them" when we take the challenge into ourselves before offering it to another. We need to ask ourselves how the challenge applies to us? How are we like that? How do we sometimes act in a similar way? Opening to the challenge ourselves before offering it to another person moves us beyond feeling superior. Any sense of superiority is separating; it polarizes. A challenge that doesn't come from separation doesn't create separation. It comes not like an arrow that wounds but an acupuncture needle that heals.

There are many situations in which some of us experience power and privilege over others. If we think we're inherently superior, we distance ourselves from them and from our centre. But if we are in essence—if we identify with our Essence-Self rather than with the outer persona of our role—we can use our power and privilege for the benefit of all. When we remember that we're branches from the same trunk, we come into a state of inner peace that supports the whole Tree of Life to flourish.

The metaphor of the forked tree means looking at life as a mirror. The Medicine Wheel represents life; it is a great mirror in which all things are reflected. All things are on the Medicine Wheel, and all things are equal on it. Everything is a mirror reflecting everything else. When you see something in another person that you don't like, look for what it reflects in you, and learn to love it. When you see something in another person that you admire, look for that quality in yourself, and learn to own it. It's part of your gift to life.

When we feel a reaction to what we see in the mirror, our work is to stay present with the uncomfortable feelings. It can be tempting to go into conflict, because we want the feelings to go away. But the way

80

of the forked tree is to process our emotions with awareness and not let them push us into war. If we want peace in our world, we need peace in our consciousness.

Being present we observe our body and breath. We remember our connection with the ground below and the sky above. We make peace with each moment. From this energy, we can then challenge, confront, or otherwise engage with what we've seen in the mirror. And the result of acting from peace in the Self is peace in the world.

In my early childhood, trees inspired me as play apparatus; now they inspire me as spiritual teachers. I am sitting in a park in London as I write this piece. Around me are all sorts of people, of all sorts of cultures, speaking all sorts of languages. And around us are all sorts of trees. Each of the humans is unique; each of the trees is unique; each of the leaves is special. Diversity is in the nature of life.

Emotions are not right or wrong; they are diversity within us. The more we embrace this inner diversity the more we can welcome diversity in the world. And as the world grows ever closer, I reflect, the time has come for us to celebrate our differences, to grow beyond "us and them" thinking and to honour wholeness in diversity.

PRACTICE: Life as a Mirror

Use this practice when something upsets or disturbs you.
It supports your emotional intelligence with other aspects of consciousness, particularly your presence, path, and heart intelligences.

First, accept your feelings. Don't deny them, but be open to harnessing them for your highest growth. Now come into stillness, and heighten your presence. Be conscious of your breath.
Accept the present moment as it is, including your feelings.
Observe your emotions. How do they feel in the body?
Notice thoughts arising, but don't get caught up in them.
Be aware of the space in which they occur. Let go of labelling or thinking about the past.

Second, when you feel more present, remind yourself that you are on a journey to the centre. Remember that you are on a path of awakening and can learn something from this situation.
You are a being of the light of the Universe. Whoever else is involved in this situation, they too are spirit, awakening in their own way.

Now connect with your heart. Take a few deep breaths while putting your attention on your heart. The heart has clarity, space, and wisdom. Let it take you beyond the surface and see the essence of the disturbance. How has this disturbed you? What does it reflect? From this heart-space, choose how to respond to the situation. How will you engage with the other?

Let this practice empower you. Becoming present reconnects you so you can see the reflection in the mirror of life. You can then harness the emotional energy for your intention, learning, and awakening.

Truth and Reconciliation

We can draw on the powers we opened in the East and Southeast to support us to go beyond "us and them" thinking. We can awaken the field of all potential within and expand our awareness through presence. By activating these aspects of consciousness, we meet life in trust and innocence and have a different effect on all around us. This is highly significant for our world, as we'll see in this section.

War or peace? Whether it's one or the other depends to a large extent on our discipline of emotion. It takes courage to be vulnerable and open; it takes presence to connect with the wholeness behind diversity; it challenges our separate identity to look in the mirror. But each effort we make as individuals, we contribute to the collective change needed. If the collective consciousness is like an ocean, groups of people make waves in it.

For example, Mahatma Gandhi and his followers made waves using non-violence and soul-force. They helped the British Empire dissolve fairly peacefully and inspired Martin Luther King's dreams to bring non-violent change in the USA. The ripples flowed on to the shores of South Africa and broke through apartheid. The end of that racist regime wasn't bloodless, but it was far from the bloodbath many expected. How did that happen?

It was partly through the emotional intelligence of the leaders of the revolution: Desmond Tutu, Nelson Mandela, and many others. Revenge is said to be sweet, but they knew it was also toxic. They acted as elders to the different racial groups and brought them together. They also worked to heal years of trauma and injustice.

Mainstream justice is largely based on retribution, but Indigenous ways of justice are more intended to restore balance. The new government of South Africa drew on Indigenous traditions to set up the Truth and Reconciliation Commission. They wanted to bring healing through a kind of national catharsis. The commission called in victims and perpetrators from all sides to face what had happened and to hear each other's emotional truth.

It's been told how an elderly woman stood before her oppressor at the Truth and Reconciliation Commission. Her oppressor had been a policeman during apartheid and had gleefully tortured and murdered the woman's son. Some years later, he had returned to her house, and she had witnessed him and colleagues brutally killing her husband.

A member of the commission asked her what she wanted: "How should justice be done to this man who has so brutally destroyed your family?"

Her first request was to be taken to the place where her husband's body had been burned so that she could gather up the dust and give his remains a decent burial.

She continued: "My husband and son were my only family. I want secondly for Mr. van der Broek to become my son. I would like for him to come twice a month to the ghetto and spend a day with me so that I can pour out on him whatever love I still have remaining within me.

"And finally," she said. "I want a third thing. I would like Mr. van der Broek to know that I offer him my forgiveness because Jesus Christ died to forgive. This was also the wish of my husband. And so, I would kindly ask someone to come to my side and lead me across the courtroom so that I can take Mr. van der Broek in my arms, embrace him, and let him know he is truly forgiven."

At this, the old woman's friends and family in the court began to sing "Amazing Grace," and the accused man fainted.

Clearly, this old woman inspired a shift of consciousness in her former oppressor. The fact that one person has a heart that big reflects well on our whole species. But each of us has the potential for the consciousness, soul-force, and ability to transform energy. This is what we are called to at this time. What do we need to grow to this level? I imagine the old woman must have opened to her own pain because only then could she have been willing to embrace the other in forgiveness. When you know suffering in yourself, you know it in the other. You have a sense of your common humanity. You empathize.

Pain is a teacher. But often we don't know how to learn from it, and many of us avoid it at all costs—perhaps because we fear it'll swallow us up. When you allow yourself to be present to your feelings, you create no resistance to them, and they pass through. Sometimes you need to express them to let them move. Avoidance makes them linger. Feeling never killed anyone, but various forms of avoidance do; thinking can be an avoidance. It takes trust and courage to be present to pain, but when you do so, you are able to hear its message and teaching. You take the learning.

We all experience loss and grief. We call these heartbreaking, but the heart doesn't really break. Love doesn't break the heart; the heart breaks open to love. The heart is our primary organ of healing. Being present to feelings with heart open, you come to a level of humanity that's beyond surface identity with this group of people or that. Presence heals prejudice. When you're not caught up in ideas about the "other," your spirit recognizes their spirit. By being present, open, and vulnerable, you access the power of transformation.

Presence is the doorway to deep listening. Deep listening can heal and restore peace to relationships. It means the listeners are present, attentive, and open—open-hearted, open-minded, open to receive. Open receptivity allows space for energy to move into, and this brings healing.

On the other hand, when we're full of argument, we're not fully listening to the other person's energy. There's no space for their energy to move. For example, when my daughter expresses a different perspective from mine, I sometimes notice myself thinking, *Yes, but . . .* —already planning how to argue back. But if I stop and tell myself to open, that shift of energy leads to resolution.

People have criticized the Truth and Reconciliation process for being too lenient or not going far enough. Several decades later, South Africa faces ongoing challenges, but it helped the country avoid the flood of blood that might have followed its revolution.

Desmond Tutu, one of the chairs of the Commission, wrote this:

Forgiving and being reconciled to our enemies or our loved ones are not about pretending that things are other than they are. . . . True reconciliation exposes the awfulness, the abuse, the hurt, the truth. It could even sometimes make things worse. It is a risky undertaking, but in the end it is worthwhile, because in the end only an honest confrontation with reality can bring real healing. Superficial reconciliation can bring only superficial healing. [11]

If we are to move beyond "us and them" thinking, heal the festering wounds across our planet, and create the culture of peace that's needed, we need more processes like this. Let the healing begin in the Self, and the wave roll on.

PRACTICE: Council of Relationship Peace

This practice is for healing any kind of relationship between two people. It is especially useful when there's been conflict and enables the two to restore peace and understanding.

First, each person prepares alone by looking within. They become present and ask themselves: "How did I help create this situation?" and "What can I learn from this?" It's important to replace the desire to "win" with the desire for learning and reconciliation.

Agree a time and space for good communication, find a quiet, neutral place without interruptions (phones on silent). One person can make it beautiful by cleaning and perhaps bringing flowers or lighting a candle. Call in the spirit of healing.

The first person states simply what happened from their point of view. The second person mirrors back what they heard (not what

86

they thought happened). The first person then speaks about how they felt as a result. This is without throwing energy at the listener; for example, actually getting angry with them. The second person then mirrors back what they heard. For example, "I hear you felt . . ."

At this point, it's helpful if the listener is able to empathize with and validate the speaker's feelings. They need to be present and open-hearted to do so. Essentially, they show that they understand the speaker's feelings. For example, "I understand your feeling of being criticized and put down when I spoke in that tone."

The listener may also check whether they've understood and whether there's anything more. Often when one person feels their feelings validated, they can release and move on.

Then reverse the process. The second person speaks about what happened from their perspective; the first speaks back what they heard, and so on.

We need to learn to be present with our own and with other people's feelings. Presence is healing. It takes time to develop the ability to listen and validate another's feelings in the middle of an emotional surge. We need to suspend judgement and embrace vulnerability to come to reconciliation. But this is powerful growth for the soul.

React or Respond

 There's a difference between reaction and response. Emotions can drive us to act on impulse; that's a reaction. Or we can connect with our centre before acting; that's a response. Our ability to respond—our "response-ability"— is an essential quality of centred consciousness.

With response, there's a space between the stimulus and the action. "Response-ability" comes from inner spaciousness. The spaciousness of presence gives you awareness to estimate the most life-enhancing response for you and those around you. In the space, you are able to access the wisdom within. Here's a story to illustrate the power of response.

The crisis came at Maddie's party. Kalima was with a group of people in the kitchen. Dale was there, too, and she was hoping they'd get talking. The magic in his eyes tied a little knot in her stomach, though she wondered what her parents would think. But there was something awkward in the air. Some people were larking around, while others were unusually subdued. Maria was taking a lot of attention, acting all loud and brazen.

Maria was her oldest friend, but now she was making fun of Kalima's clothes. "Honestly, Kalima, how could anyone wear that to a party? Looks like you just stepped off your old lady's washing line."

Everybody laughed, but Kalima's cheeks flushed. If there was anything she hated, it was being mocked. She felt the familiar urge to withdraw. She wanted to be invisible again, but she also knew that was an old pattern. Here was a chance to change it and be free.

Kalima knew that, deep down, Maria was just as shy as she was.

They'd actually been friends from an early age, but there'd been tension between them recently. Why was Maria being cruel? Why did she want to expose Kalima's weakness?

There'd been plenty of humiliation in Kalima's childhood. She'd been laughed at for getting angry and teased for shyness. But things had started to change when she was nearly 18. Her parents had needed to spend time abroad, and she'd been sent to live with Aunt Zeynep.

Zeynep worked in the Human Resources Department of a large company. She was interested in personal development and was training to be a life coach. She had two younger children, and Kalima helped care for them. But Zeynep had a way of comforting them that surprised Kalima. When they were upset, she would validate their feelings instead of trying to get them to just get over it.

She encouraged Kalima to take a similar approach: "We all have to soothe ourselves when we're upset," she said. "The best way to start is being present with feelings and let them pass. It's good to make friends with yourself."

With Zeynep's support, Kalima began to unravel the tangle of her own emotional strands. Zeynep encouraged her not to put herself down because of her feelings. Kalima found that being present with them enabled her to understand them better. She still felt embarrassed by emotions at times, but she trusted Zeynep enough to share how she felt with her. She came to see that hiding from vulnerability made it worse. As Zeynep said, "There's a power in being vulnerable." It felt exciting and empowering.

After a while she had joined a yoga class and learned a form of meditation. She'd found this so helpful she'd wanted Maria to join, too. Maria had refused, and the harder Kalima had tried to persuade her, the more resistant Maria had become.

Now, at the party, it came to her that Maria's hostility had started from then. Perhaps Maria felt that Kalima had abandoned her in some way. Maybe her aggression came out of loneliness.

Kalima knew that if she didn't say anything, she'd go away feeling humiliated. She felt the rising surge of anger and the desire to attack. But she didn't want to make things worse or embarrass herself in front of her friends. She remembered the meditation she'd been doing that morning, the breath going in and out, and recalled Zeynep's words about the power of vulnerability.

"I know," she said. "Actually, I find my clothes really embarrassing. But I wouldn't have been here for hours if I'd gone home to change. I wanted to be here for Maddie."

Maddie herself responded. "I don't care what you're wearing. Fact is you made the effort to get here, and I'm so glad to see you."

Often we react because we feel threatened. The limbic part of our brain notices threat and produces a flood of hormones that make us want to fight to defend ourselves. This can be because we perceive a threat in a social situation. We can reassure and remind ourselves that we have personal power. Our power comes from our centre and connection with the Universe.

We connect with it through presence.

Vulnerability is an expression of power. It means revealing ourselves for who we are, in our innocence. Kalima knew that if she accepted her feelings and was open, others would see her real-ness. It took courage, but it changed the mood of the party.

Later in the evening, Dale came up to her. "That was really cool the way you handled Maria." Kalima felt vulnerable, but she stayed open. It enabled Dale to reveal more of himself, and it created a rapport between them.

Reactivity is higher when we're stressed. Where does stress come from? It can seem to come from the situation out there in the world, but often the only place we can do anything about it is inside. We can make peace with our feelings, no matter how difficult they are. We can reassure ourselves and accept the present moment as it is. Stress comes from wanting things to be different from how they are. Accepting them makes peace with the present moment.

We all have emotional patterning structured in us. But we can heal and change the structure with awareness and attention. Accepting the moment gives us space to pause and respond. "Response-ability" opens our heart to choice. We can then choose our words and actions with the awareness of what they may lead to.

Much of our emotional patterning is established during childhood. It comes from the energies of people around us — parents or guardians, other relatives, teachers, and peer group — and from how we interpreted those energies. Images from religion or the media also have a strong influence. As children we absorb these messages and they shape our mental structure. As adults we have the choice to change these structures so that we can continue to grow and expand. The practice below supports this process.

We initiated this journey in the East by activating our essence as beings of light with access to unlimited potential. In the Southeast, we added that we have perceptual consciousness and the power of stillness. In the South, we've opened our emotional consciousness: We've seen how to use our East and Southeast energies to guide our emotional power on this journey of growth. In the next chapter, we'll explore intentional consciousness: the power to direct our energies and shape our destiny.

PRACTICE: Presence and Personal Power

Whenever you are challenged in a social situation, stay present. Pause and breathe.

Don't let your feelings push you into a reaction or get caught up in your thoughts about them. Instead, notice the effect of the feelings on your body and breath.

Observe your feelings without judging them good or bad. Notice how they affect your thinking. Notice the urge to get caught up in your emotional pattern, even though it may be painful and unpleasant. It can be like an energy vortex that wants to suck your awareness into it.

But remember that this challenge is also an opportunity to restructure your emotional patterning. You can grow your emotional stability and ability to respond in this moment. When you observe your emotional patterns, you are no longer totally identified with them. This space around them gives you the awareness to see deeply into them and ask what is needed for healing.

Now direct your attention to the heart. Feel your heart, and choose how to respond. When you bring emotion through the heart, it is more likely to lead to a life-affirming result than if you react.

If you find that you have already acted out your reaction, have compassion for yourself. No judgement. But try to have compassion for the other people involved, too. When you have time and space, look back into this incident to observe how you were triggered. Imagine how you might have responded. Imagining your response creates a new neural pathway.

When we know the kinds of situation that trigger our reaction, we can approach them with more presence, space, and awareness. This takes dedication and training but helps us keep a connection with the centre of the Self. Then we're able to express more of our personal power in the world.

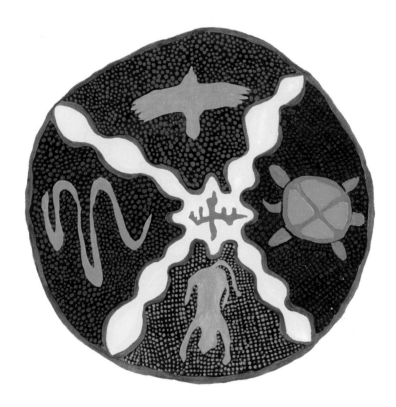

Celebrating Wholeness in Diversity

PATH

4

Southwest: Path

Our life is a journey. Where we have been, where we are now, and where we are going: that's our path. It gives us a sense of identity and of the unique gift we are to life.

On the journey of this book, we have awakened the unlimited potential of the creative (East), heightened awareness of the present (Southeast) and grown in trust of our Self and feelings (South). Here in the Southwest, we remember our path as sacred spirit.

The past exists as memory, and the stories we tell about our experiences are forms of memory. How we tell these stories shapes our sense of identity, and our sense of identity is fundamental to how we move in life. On the surface, our identity is represented by the name and details in our passport, but our true identity is deeper and vaster. It's from this depth that our sacred path emerges—from the mystery of Self.

Everything in life is embedded with its essence-identity at a deep level. If you hold a seed in your hand, that seed already has its essence-identity and destiny within it. Its destiny is to grow into fullness as that particular plant, not as anything else. An acorn won't grow into a beech, banyan, or baobab; it can only become an oak.

Each of us has come into life on purpose, with a unique destiny. Path awareness means remembering this. It means recalling our essence-identity and following the sacred path to our destination. Each of us plays a part in the song of the Universe, a part that no one else can play. We are here to awaken consciousness, each in our own way, and to carry unique gifts into the world, each in our own way.

When we remember our deepest sense of identity, we come into alignment with life. This enables us to stay focused on our path and move towards our destiny. It contributes to the resolution of the global crisis.

The "seat" of path awareness is the brain, the principal organ of memory. The brain also gives us the faculties of reason and analysis. But we can become so busy with the chatter of verbal thought that we come to totally identify with it. We then forget the depth of who we are, get confused, and lose our way. Life can seem like a maze in which we've lost the thread. Path awareness is finding the thread again and remembering our sacred path.

Learning to manage thought supports this remembrance. It helps us find and follow our path. **Secret of the Aztecs** is about how to focus thought and train ourselves to harness its power.

It's easy to forget what we've come into life for. **Fingerprints of the Gods** is about listening for the whispers and yearnings of Spirit. When we hear them, our true purpose emerges, and our sacred path unfolds.

No one can tell another person what they should do with their life. **What Is My Purpose?** tells my son's story of finding his way when he was lost. He used the ancient practice of vision quest, going deep into the wilderness to listen for the voice of Spirit.

The Golden Threads of Destiny tells another vision quest story, one of my own. It explores how our individual threads of destiny weave together to produce this magnificent "dream" we call life.

Secret of the Aztecs

Our thoughts have a profound effect on our experience. Learning to manage them helps us stay focused on our path. While dozing one afternoon, I went into a reverie and received a message about this.

An Aztec princess, her dark hair shimmering with quetzal feathers, white dress decorated with turquoise. Her brown eyes flash a smile, and I know I am meant to climb the steps of the temple with her.

We mount each step mindfully, in a dignified procession, and come to the top of the first level.

We're on a pyramid. I look out to the four directions. There are people below, sky above, forest all around, and the sea beyond.

We start to climb higher, and I see the topmost step is purple. I sense that I'm to be initiated. As I reach the purple step, I am flooded with light—refined and shimmering light. Before me is an obsidian bowl filled with water. I kneel to look in the bowl. I see the reflection of the moon with clouds scudding across it, and I am touched by beauty. I hear her voice in my ear:

"All life is a dream; all thought shapes the dream."

And with that I began to feel my body in bed again, and realized I was in England in the 21st century. I remembered a Chinese sage, Chuang Tzu, dreaming he was a butterfly but wondering if he might be a butterfly dreaming he was a man.[12]

I got up and went down to the kitchen. Everything seemed solid enough. My house was similar to the way I remembered it before going to bed. I couldn't walk through the wall, and things didn't change when I looked at them, as they do in night dreams. This was clearly waking reality, and if it was a dream, it was different from a sleeping dream.

"All thought shapes the dream." Her words echoed in my mind. I'd known the truth of this statement a long time. Once when I'd been unhappy, my mother had cheered me up with homespun wisdom:

> *"Two men looked out of the prison bars,*
> *One saw mud and the other saw stars."*

After she told me this, I changed my thoughts and started looking for stars and positivity. It had caused the heaviness about my heart to lift. And authorities with more scientific kudos than Mum have said similar things.

In *Molecules of Emotion*, pioneering scientist Candace Pert wrote about how thoughts affect the body. The "molecules of emotion" are neuropeptides, chemicals produced primarily in the brain but also in most tissues in the body. These chemical messengers carry information that affects our thinking, feeling, digestion, and nervous system.[13]

In *The Brain that Changes Itself*, Norman Doidge, a psychiatrist and neuroscientist, wrote: "Every thought alters the physical state of your brain synapses at a microscopic level."[14]

Thoughts mould the cracks, crevices, and crenellations of our grey jelly, the brain. They shape its topography—opening and closing synapses, linking and separating neurons, as water sculpts a landscape, creating gullies and riverbeds to flow down. Some thought channels become so deeply etched that our reactions are automatic and take place without conscious agreement. But we don't need to be run by subconscious thought patterns; we have the power to change our inner landscape, if we choose.

Mind and body are not separate. They are both elements of the human Self, along with emotion and spirit. Together these four elements of Self create our experience, our reality, our sacred dream of life. This was known to the ancient Mexicans.

The body isn't here just to take the brain to its next meeting. The brain plays an important part in thinking, but it is not the only organ involved. Within the body are other energy centres, such as the sex organs, womb, and solar plexus, the heart, voice, and sense organs. Each of these generates various kinds of thought; gut feeling, for example, or heart knowing. And each of them receives thought from the Self and from the Universe.

All parts of the body are interrelated and have consciousness of various kinds. We're often unaware of them because our attention is occupied with brain-thought. If our brain is too busy, it becomes difficult to notice these more subtle realms of consciousness. It's like having a radio or TV constantly blaring out, and only when we turn the volume down, by getting present, can we hear anything else.

When our waking mind is asleep and we go into REM sleep, our body-mind expresses itself in dreams. But we can also be aware of the body-mind while we're awake. The body-mind is a vast field of intuitive intelligence that "knows" directly and "thinks" in a dreamy way. This is in contrast with the repetitive patterns of verbal thought so typical of the brain-mind.

Since thought has such a pervasive influence on the Self ("all thought shapes the dream"), what can we do to influence thought? Awareness arises from the practices of the East, Southeast, and South. It gives us the power to choose thought that supports the beauty of our dream. This is a step in learning to command our energy and dream consciously. Then "my" dream can help "our" dream come back into harmony with Earth's dream.

Thoughts are like clouds drifting across the clear sky of our mind, hoping to catch our attention. "I" am not the thoughts but the sky, the field of consciousness in which thoughts occur. Some thoughts lead us off our path. We can choose to let them go by and return to our focus of attention, or we can deliberately choose particular thoughts, knowing how they may affect our state of energy-consciousness. But choice comes from awareness; awareness from presence; and presence from directing attention to the present moment. The body is always present in the here and now, but our attention can sometimes be miles away.

Experience teaches us what happens when particular thoughts occur and take hold. They trigger a cascade of neuropeptides that flood our system with emotion, like wind whipping up waves on the still surface of a lake. They take us into states we don't want or haven't consciously chosen such as "bad moods." It's easier to interrupt these thoughts at the first ripple, because once the waves are raging it takes more effort to still them and find our way back to the centre.

Every thought is a form of prayer because the unconscious is always listening. Even "little" thoughts of the subconscious and unconscious have an effect on us and life. When we say things to ourselves like *I can't do this*, that thought reinforces our inability. If instead we say "I'm seeking a way" or "I'm open to learning," we open the door of possibility, the portal to the field of all potential.

The Universe is benevolent, and life affirms thought that affirms life. Our most powerful thoughts are life-affirming and backed by as much of our focused intention as we can muster. When we bring the surface waters of our mind into stillness, we are able to drop power-thoughts into the depths. There they reverberate around the inner recesses of the Infinite Self.

Remembering our identity as spirit-expressions of the Infinite Vastness, we allow the universal life force to flow through us. In this expanded state of consciousness, it's easy to notice diminishing thoughts that aren't in alignment with it. Your expanded thoughts create a great web of consciousness that catches any belittling thoughts like a net catching fish.

Awareness of diminishing thoughts gives you the ability to interrupt and replace them. An interruption can be as simple as a conscious breath, directing your attention to the present, or changing your body position, or it can be more elaborate.

Changing the dream takes perseverance, but it's worth the effort; even a small change in our consciousness can be a major benefit to the world. One of the symbols I use to evoke that dedication in myself is the image of the Aztec priestess. She is a loving guide in my inner world, one who supports my work of healing myself and changing the dream.

PRACTICE: Sculpting Your Landscape of Thought

This practice reconditions your thinking and helps you maintain an expanded state of consciousness. It takes a few minutes and can be repeated three times a day. You emanate your prayer-thoughts into the Universe and through all the nooks and crannies of consciousness. This creates new channels for thought-energy.

Start by sitting quietly, with your eyes closed. Take 10 deep breaths.

With each breath, relax deeper. Release any concerns from the external world. Your mind is like a well or deep lake. Allow its surface waters to become still and calm. Connect with the depths.

Now remind yourself of your essence of identity. You are the Universe, life force, consciousness itself, born in human form. Evoke this with images and feelings. Use images that evoke a feeling of essential love. For example, I use images of people I've loved and felt loved by, animals such as my dog, and magical places. You could also use such images as a rainbow, fire, the moon, a rose, and so on. Let this feeling resonate through your body and energy centres: brain, senses, throat, heart, solar plexus, womb, and sex.

Now follow this image-feeling with a verbal thought-phrase that empowers you and reminds you of the essence of identity; for example, "I am loving awareness," "I am spirit with unlimited potential," or "I am a sacred child of Mother Earth." Repeat this phrase 10 times.

Close this practice by counting down from 10 to 1. Smile and open your eyes. You are now ready to engage with the outer world again.

Fingerprints of the Gods

 The second part of path awareness is remembering our deepest sense of identity. The DNA in our cells holds the essential blueprint of our uniqueness, because the essence of identity is embedded in cellular memory. By remembering our Self-Essence we can connect with the uniqueness of our path.

If you look closely at the palms of your hands you see unique patterns. Your fingerprints are distinct and special. No other person has this configuration of whirls, swirls, and arches; neither has any person in the past, and nor (as far as we know) will any person in the future. Not even identical twins have the same pattern. The same goes for the prints on your feet, the iris patterns of your eyes, and the biometrics of your voice. Each of them is evidence for your singular uniqueness. There's never been anyone like you, nor will there ever be again. You can't be duplicated. Your place in history is assured.

Life is full of uniqueness. It expresses itself in a myriad of diverse forms. No two things are exactly the same. To the casual eye two blades of grass may look the same, but observe closely enough and you'll see they're different. Every tree is unique. Every fire is unique. Every dog is unique—the prints on dogs' noses are as distinct as the prints on human hands and feet.

And these patterns continue through life. Each of us was born with our prints; we've grown with them and will die with them. Our essential identity is embedded within us, as it is with all beings. The seed carries the pattern of what it will become.

"Who am I?" is both an easy and impossible question to answer. It's easy to label ourselves with a name or fill in a form with the typical details: date of birth, nationality, sex, and so on. But this is only the outer form; the true essence of our identity is embedded much deeper, in our DNA and cellular memory. The deep truth of who we are is a mystery that cannot be completely defined; there is always more to discover. Nevertheless, asking ourselves the question opens us to new levels of self-knowing.

Life is a sacred dream, and each of us is a vital part of it. Each of us is needed for the whole. Our purpose is to become who we've come here to be. We're here to awaken, but each of us must find our way of doing so. It is a lifelong voyage of discovery to uncover and express our Self as a unique creation of the Universe. But how do we find our path? Who have we come here to be? What is the essence of our identity? And how can we nurture the seed of our essence to maturity?

Life offers us signposts in various ways. We draw to ourselves unexpected challenges or experiences that touch us deeply. They are opportunities to learn and unfold our path, but we are free to choose how to interpret and respond to them. Self-authority means we are the authors of our lives. Sometimes we struggle with challenges for ages, and it can take many years' hindsight to see their deeper message. Looking for the teaching behind experiences supports us to find the way forward.

We need to listen to the deep longing of our soul. We connect with our individuality through memory, particularly of childhood before we were completely domesticated. We may find clues here about our path. Do we remember activities in which we were completely absorbed, lost in the eternal present and filled with joy?

Dreams also offer us messages. For example, in dreams, a building can symbolize the Self. Around the beginning of my Medicine training, I dreamed of my house. The outside looked like my house in waking consciousness, but great changes were underway inside. The builders had taken out the interior walls and were rearranging the rooms. They were even changing the staircase.

As my training unfolded, I worked to change the structures of my consciousness by re-examining assumptions, beliefs, and images that I'd been holding. I needed to break down the walls to allow my sense of Self to evolve and become closer to the inner mystery expressed by the prints on my palms.

What holds us back from walking the sacred path of our individuality? One of the inner chains that holds many of us back (including myself) is fear of "What will other people think?" It is a helpful conditioning—to notice people's feedback and understand social rules. But we also need to free ourselves enough to break the rules if they hold back our self-expression.

The psychologist Carl Jung used to hold the question: "What is my myth?" Jung experienced a difficult period during his forties after he broke with Sigmund Freud. Not only did he lose Freud, who'd been a mentor and father figure for him, but also most of his friends and acquaintances. The book he'd published was declared rubbish, and he was dismissed as a mystic. He felt lost and went into emotional and psychic turmoil.

In the darkness of this time, he remembered that as a boy he'd loved to play with stones, building little houses and castles with mud and stones. He felt there was vitality in this memory. "This small boy is still around," he thought, "and possesses a creative life that I lack."

In spite of feeling resistance, he made himself play with stones again and went down to the lakeshore to make tiny villages. He realized that he was performing a ritual expression of his unconscious and was making a bridge between his inner world and physical form.

Working with stone became Jung's therapy. He came to see stone as a symbol of Divine Oneness. It helped him come out of the turmoil: He said he was no longer "held captive in the magic mountain." He began to express his psyche by building a primitive hut. It was the result of his urge to give form to images from the inner layers of his psyche, and in time, this building evolved into a tower and then a two-storey family home. He later added a second tower. Eventually, with the help of his architect son, Franz, the building evolved even more, into an enchanted castle.

As Jung himself explained:

After my wife's death I felt an inner obligation to become what I myself am. To put it in the language of the Bollingen house, I suddenly realized that the central section, which crouched so low, so hidden, was myself! I could no longer hide myself behind the "maternal" and "spiritual" towers, so I added an upper storey which represented myself. Earlier, I would not have been able to do this. I would have regarded it as presumptuous self-emphasis. Now it signifies an extension of consciousness achieved in old age. With that the building was complete. [15]

By then Jung was internationally renowned as a scientist, thinker, and writer. But when some visitors from overseas came to his village for a visit and asked a local for directions, the villager had never heard of him as a famous psychologist: "Jung? Do you mean the old stonemason?"

Space was very important to Jung. In later years, he used to hang out "mood flags" to signal to people whether he was receiving visitors or not. Space is an important aspect of finding our uniqueness—space from activity, from visitors, from social media. In the next section, we'll explore a practice of giving ourselves space and time alone to find our path.

PRACTICE: Daily Intention

Early in the day, take some moments to call forward the question, "What is the essence of my identity?" It can help to step outside to do this. Remind yourself of your relationship with the Universe—the earth below and sky above. You are a unique expression of life and are here for a unique purpose.

What is needed for your awakening? What pattern of thought do you need this day? From this communion with Self and life, allow an intention for the day to arise, and trust that it will be in alignment with your life purpose. Speak this intention clearly so that it reverberates in the depths of your being.

You may also write it down and carry it in your pocket or create something to remind yourself of it through the day.

Late in the day, note down what you've learned in a journal that's specifically for this journey that you're on. Write your observations (no judgement is needed). Did you stay on your path? Did you follow your intention? If you were distracted, how did it happen? How did you manage your energy? Did you react or respond to challenges?

Reminding ourselves of our unique intention and tracking ourselves like this are powerful methods to deepen path-intelligence. And these moments of twilight—the threshold times after waking up or shortly before sleep—are powerful moments to connect with the depth of our being.

What Is My Purpose

Managing our thinking and focusing our intention are two aspects of path-awareness. Now let's explore the practice of questing. Questing means listening to the longing of your soul. It is an old way of aligning with purpose. People have quested alone in nature on every continent and at all times in history, among them Moses, Merlin, Muhammad, Mahavira, Jesus, and Buddha. It's a powerful way to connect with our centre and find our way.

To enter the silence of one's soul in the heart of nature allows us to reconnect with the mystery of all life and for this to become our greatest teacher. When we immerse ourselves in being, we connect with inner resources and with the depth of who we are. It brings regeneration and a renewal of our sense of purpose.

I have been on many quests and have witnessed many others in this deep process. One of them was with my son Felix, who went on vision quest as part of his rite of passage towards manhood.

Here's the story of his quest.

We headed north. For two days after we'd left the northerly city of Helsinki, the needle on my compass pointed straight ahead, through the windscreen of our van. North, and yet further north, past countless lakes and numberless trees, until late the second evening, well into Arctic Lapland, we stopped in the half-night. It was a little past the time of the midnight sun, but the sun didn't dip far below the horizon, and sunset blended into sunrise. The light was eerie.

Then we walked—away from modernity and into the magic forest that girdles the earth at these latitudes.

We were seven. We had come for shamanic walking, my son for
his rite of passage. There was nobody else here; occasionally, the signs
left by reindeer herders, but no other humans. The presence of Spirit
was strong. We placed our feet mindfully on the moss—the moss that
seemed to lie as thick as the years in this primeval place.

After walking for two days, we came to a ridge where a hawk was
nesting and camped nearby. It was here that Felix would go for his
vision quest.

Rites of passage are an ancient practice that would help restore the
present culture to balance if we revived them. As adolescents, we want
self-authority but don't grow into it simply by breaking rules or taking risks
without a structure to hold us. We need processes held by communities
that mark and acknowledge each person's growth.

Ideally, an adolescent rite of passage marks the transition from child
to adult, from being cared for by others to taking responsibility for
yourself. It may not complete this transition in itself but activates deep
levels of the psyche to make the crossing possible. It strengthens a young
person's relationship with the Self, so they can access the inner resources
with which to meet Life's inevitable challenges. It helps them come into
balance, and balanced individuals make a balanced society.

Felix had been unhappy at school. Alienated, he felt he didn't belong.
When you're on the threshold between child and adult, getting on with
your peers is all-important, but his tactic of playing the fool didn't win
him any friends. He told me later he'd thought of suicide.

Perhaps it was this suffering that led him to agree to a rite of passage.
He recounted:

On my vision quest a great many things happened in a short time
before I took flight. For the first hour or two I was just setting up the
circle in which I'd stay. I prepared my fireplace and got wood for it.
I noticed the fire was burning a lot of fuel quickly—probably because
of the wind blowing fresh oxygen in all the time.

I took my T-shirt off and hung it on a pole to show me where my camp was, while I went to get more wood. I knew something had happened, so I looked back and saw my T-shirt had fallen into the fire. I ran back and picked up the pole, but the shirt was on fire. I waved it in the air but realized it was the wrong thing to do, so I let it go back into the fire.

A dark cloud came over. I could tell it was going to rain, so I put my stuff under a tree. Rain it did, but that wasn't all. There was intense thunder and lightning and strong wind. The wind blew the trees as if they were blades of grass, not the strong pine trees I had seen moments before. I thought I might be in danger near the trees, so I ran out of the forest towards a copse of silver birch.

This is where the Power-That-Is came into play. I asked what I should do, and the message came: Go back to your area. When I did, the rain got harder and the thunder louder. Put your towel on your head. I did so, and that was what stopped me getting so wet. I tried counting the seconds between thunder and lightning. At this point, there was no gap, and I was probably the most scared I have ever been in my entire life. I was crying and begging the spirit not to do this to me.

Then I was wondering why I was so scared of my own death. I realized I wanted to see the world and my friends and family and to experience things. This I yelled out to the Power-That-Is. Then after commanding Him not to do this to me, I pondered, Why not? I was just one in billions of people, so why not just toy with me? It wouldn't make much difference. I stopped crying and said this. I also said that I would be very grateful if He were to spare me. The thunder and lightning went, and the sun came out. And then a bird of prey screeched and landed on top of the tree next to me, and I received a message: I have spared you, but you must teach others that life is worth living. That bird stayed with me for a long time.

I looked over the ridge, and there was an enormous stag with large antlers standing about 20 metres away. It felt me see it, and it ran to the west, then stopped, looked at me, and ran South. When I had run out of my circle, I had poured water over my fire to extinguish it, and yet when I came back . . . it relit itself.

I was so surprised by this. But I know that when the stag ran away, the fire was out. This was when I ran. I thought the lightning strike had been a test, and I had failed it. It was only later that I realized this was going to change my life.

Felix came back into camp crying because he thought he'd failed. The rest of us were drying things out after the storm. He told his story to Chris, his guide for the rite, and in doing so realized that he'd received the Medicine he'd been seeking. His journey had connected him with the resources of the deep psyche and the mythic level of being.

Not everyone has such dramatic experiences while questing, but by leaving our usual routines and going on retreat in places of primeval power, we open important life questions deeply. We can ask ourselves such questions at any time, but ordinary thinking won't allow them to fully flower; we honour them by approaching them in expanded states of consciousness. We also become more conscious of the mysterious force of intention and of our unique path to the centre.

In the years immediately after his quest, Felix carried the message that "Life is worth living" to many of his troubled peer group. Now he lives in China, and when I asked him what his quest meant to him he said: "I know I'm the only person who can make me happy—and just having that thought makes me happy."

We came here on purpose. We are here to awaken, and each of us has a particular part to play in the movement of consciousness.

PRACTICE: Solo Quest

To quest into your purpose is to give yourself a gift. First, allocate a period—anything from a few hours to several days—to step out of usual routines. Then protect that time and space. Don't let it be eroded by demands from your everyday life.

Before you go solo, take time to become clear about your intention. Contemplate this, and allow your question to emerge. What is the question that most deeply crosses your life at this time? You could hold a question like "What is my unique gift?" or "How can I best contribute to healing the relationship between humanity and the rest of life on Earth?" Write this intention down.

Create a power object to hold your intention. For example, you could find a stick, whittle it, and decorate it with lengths of yarn. Create it mindfully, with full attention.

Take this object with you when you go out. Find a spot in nature where you can be alone and uninterrupted. You may like to make a circle around you, your personal Medicine Wheel. You can mark this with stones or sticks, for example. Leave any portable electronic devices or means of entertainment at home. Take only what you need to be reasonably comfortable. If you choose to take your phone in case of emergency, have it switched off.

This is time for being, not doing. Allow space to simply be with yourself without distractions. Boredom won't kill you. If you feel bored, allow yourself to be present with that feeling. You will become more intimate with yourself and the mystery of each moment.

Be quiet and receptive. Sit in the circle. Be aware of the different aspects of yourself, and listen to what they say about your question. Reflect on your life experience. Are there any lessons from the past or childhood experiences that inform you about your path?

It would be ideal to have support from someone in preparing for this solo time. Ask them to hold you in their thoughts while you are out and welcome you when you come back from your quest. You can tell them your story.

The Golden Threads
of Destiny

I awaken from a doze. I have been fasting and questing for several days, sitting in nature, listening to the voices of the stream. Its white water falls and froths over rocks, bubbling into the pool in front of me. It flows down among the trees to my right. The trees are cloaked with ferns and lichen; the stones look like velvet gnomes huddling in coats of moss. I am enfolded by verdant wildness, and my soul is nurtured by the stillness of elemental beings.

It already seems I've been here a long time, but when I complete my quest, it'll be a memory and will seem like a dream. Many cultures have seen life as a kind of dream. In Medicine, it's called the Sacred Dream of Life. Everything in life is part of this; everything is dreaming in its own way—rocks, lizards, humans. Each of us carries a unique piece of this sacred dream, a part needed by the whole. A vision quest is a way for us to clarify our part, our piece of the sacred dream.

When you go into the wilds and stop eating for a few days, your thoughts drop into deeper rhythms. You become attuned to the cycles by which nature lives, and the border between "me" and "not-me" is less distinct.

I feel like I'm dreaming with the beings around me—the water, the yellow gorse flowers, the breeze caressing my hair. I imagine the dreaming of trees: breathing but once in 24 hours, writhing their branches into the sky, spreading leaves and dropping them year after year. We must be like little fireflies to them. I dream of eternal cycles of growth and decay: bracket fungus eating birch, lichen consuming rock. I see the heads of dragons in old dry sticks. Everything is in flux, cycling and recycling, energy flowing in and out of form.

A wilderness quest connects you with the world as it was when humans emerged. It awakens cellular memory of your core essence, and your sense of Self expands beyond the everyday idea of who you are. From this perspective you quest into life questions of importance such as "Who am I?" and "Where am I going?" Every one of my quests has taken me deeper into these questions and filled my life with meaning. But my intention this time is to look not only at my direction but at the collective direction of humanity. How does "my" dream weave into "our" dream?

When I am in my house, there can be the thought that I *should* be getting on with something. But here that voice is silent. Here there is nothing to be done, nowhere to go, nobody to become; thinking isn't really needed. There is only the eternal simplicity of being with each moment. I am at peace.

You can learn from the minutiae. I have been gazing into the mirror of a still pool, watching the world of water boatmen and pond-skaters, rapt in fascination and love for these little creatures. They move on the surface and seem to be playing "chase me" or "tag" with each other. They live in two dimensions; there's no up or down in their world, only the horizontal. I wonder how aware I am of other dimensions. There have been times when I've lived only on the surface, but now I resolve to live the vertical axis, too; the heights and depths of the inner dimension, consciousness.

At times, my internal dialogue goes quiet, and I find myself filled with the sound of flowing water. At other times, the chatter of thought flows as ceaselessly as the stream. But whether my mind is busy or still like a pool of clear water, underneath there's something eternal—the field of consciousness itself, as ancient as the grey granite around me. It is through the field that I know my interconnection with all things, and through this knowing that I feel my Essence-Self. Feeling the Essence-Self, I become clear about my sacred path and who I've come here to be.

The sun comes out and lights up the land around me. Liquid pearls of dew spangle the grass, sparkling with colour. I notice a spider's web gilded with light: it reminds me that all things are connected through an invisible web of light. I know my kinship with all Life. And my destiny is to awaken and live this knowing. My remembrance of this will help others to remember. The water that passes is connected with all water: with clouds and rain, seas and ocean, with icecap and steam, even with the water within each of us. I too am part of the flowing of life, the river of consciousness that flows through us from ancestors long ago to descendants many generations later. It flows on, and we will remember our relationship with all life again.

I reflect that there was a time when all people lived within nature. We were all tribal people, and everyone breathing today has tribal ancestors. In many places, our ancestors learned Earth's teaching of relationship through sitting on the ground in deep presence. They realized that they were related to all of Earth's offspring. They knew that they were part of her dream and that each one of them held a unique piece of the dream.

Some of my ancestors were of the Celtic, Anglo-Saxon, and Norse culture that flourished in Europe over a thousand years ago. As in most Indigenous cultures, they held that everything was alive, that all energy has consciousness. Theirs was a mystical landscape enchanted with vitality, magic, and meaning. The forests, streams, and hills were imbued with spiritual energies, such as elves, dwarves, and giants. They honoured the land, sea, and sky; they hallowed the sun, moon, and stars. The Universe was filled with life force, and no one was separate from it.

The Anglo-Saxons knew that all things are interrelated. Their image was that all things are connected by invisible fibres of energy in the "web of wyrd." *Wyrd* was the Anglo-Saxon name for the web of destiny behind the material world, and they likened it to a piece of weaving with innumerable threads, a fabric of huge complexity. The weavers were the three wyrd sisters who sat at the foot of the Tree of Life, spinning the threads of each person's destiny and interweaving them with others. According to one poem, the invisible fibres were golden:

"They stretched out the strings of gold
Fastened them under the hall of the moon." [16]

So my destiny and yours, dear reader, are like threads woven together, and these words are like a knot in the vast shimmering tapestry.

Wyrd means that what happens in life is the natural consequence of what has happened before. Our world is the way it is because that is the way we've dreamed it.

But we have the power to change the dream. We are not the passive victims of wyrd, but we can influence it with the power of intention. We harness this power by focusing thought and emotion and awakening our intimacy with Self and Universe. When we feel rooted in connection with all life, we can trust the meaning behind events. When we see the teaching behind events, we can harvest the learning of past experience and create something new.

In essence, we are beings made of light and have creative, sensory, emotional, and intentional consciousness. The next chapter opens our healing and sustaining consciousness.

PRACTICE: Dreaming the Golden Threads

We are co-creating the Sacred Dream of Life. In this practice, you hold the lens that there are subtle patterns beneath the surface of daily life; that everything and everyone is weaving their own thread of destiny into the great tapestry. You can set this lens as part of your intention in the morning and then look through it as you review in the evening.

Set this intention by recognizing that there is a thread of destiny running through your life and that you can uncover it by listening for the voice of your spirit. What is that you yearn for, deep down? Is there anything you can do to align with it today? You can also bring forward thoughts such as these:: I am the author of my life. As I move, I am calling things to me through the web. Whatever happens—whether events are pleasant or challenging—they offer me opportunities to awaken and empower myself.

As you go about your day, hold this lens in your consciousness. It will affect how you meet all of the energies that come to you.

You will be more consciously connected with the centre of the Self and have better access to the inner resources with which to meet life.

At the end of the day, look back at what you experienced. Consider: What can I learn from this, and how is it connected with my path? You may or may not have an immediate insight. Sometimes, it takes a longer time to see the teaching. But holding the question opens the possibility of fresh realization.

Hold compassion for yourself and others. Everyone is on a learning journey. Each of us is a thread in the great tapestry of life. There is no need for judgement.

Walking Our Sacred Path

HEALING

West: Healing

On the Medicine Wheel, West is the direction of physical structure. In the Universe, this means Earth and the planets; in the human, it means our body. Earth gives us substance for our bodies and the material things that sustain us: food, tools, shelter, and clothing. Our bodies come from the earth, and to the earth they return.

Opposite is the East, the direction of sun, stars, and Spirit. Across the East–West axis is the union of sun and earth, light and matter, essence and structure. Birth and death, form and formless—these things are not separate. They are parts of the great circle of life.

The body is divine. It houses the spirit. It is not separate from the spirit; the idea that they are separate has had a huge impact on our culture, but it is only an idea. When we realize—when we "make real" or "make part of our reality"—that both body and spirit are of the light, this goes a long way towards healing ourselves and healing our relationship with the planet. Through this realization, we honour the body and the earth, and open to their wisdom.

We can draw on the opposite direction—the creative—to support our body. When we awaken our unlimited potential and oneness with the Universe, we activate the power to heal and sustain ourselves. We can use the power of imagination to visualize wholeness and evoke health. Equally, we honour the divine by caring for the body-temple, our sacred container for this experience of life on Earth.

The energy centre in the west is the womb, or *ki* (chi) area, a little below the navel. Many traditions recognize this power centre, calling it the "hara," "onepoint," or "lower dantien." Breathing into this centre vitalizes the will and helps us hear the wisdom within. Matter is the womb in which we live and grow. We are of the formless, but we come into form to experience life. At the subatomic level, matter is composed of far more space than particles. The space is an energy field that holds particles together so that we experience it as solid. But matter itself is of the formless.

Because it is so commonplace, we think we understand what matter is. But do we really? **All Energy Has Consciousness** takes us into the mystery of matter. As we recognize this mystery, we deepen our respect for life. Deepening respect is a foundation for the power of the west in us and for meeting our global challenges.

The Dynamic Dance of Opposites expands on this theme of respect and introduces another attribute of the west: balance. It shows that introspection and intuition can teach us how to nurture and balance our Self.

A third step of conscious relationship with matter is to recognize its power to sustain us in life. This sustaining power is the life force that heals us when we're ill or have an injury. There are many ways to activate this healing power. One that we'll explore here is through our relationship with the four primary elements on Earth: fire, water, earth, and air. **The Four Elements** explores these principal forces and how our relationship with them mobilizes our healing.

The fourth step on our journey in the west is to face into the mystery of death, because life and death are a circle of wholeness. Fully realizing that our physical form will dissolve and return to the earth deepens our respect and care for it. **Death as an Ally** looks into this spiritual relationship with death and how it supports our journey of expanding consciousness.

All Energy Has Consciousness

On this stage of our journey, we need to open as fully as possible to the physical realm. The first part of this opening is to the mystery within the physical. The mainstream paradigm views the physical as just dead matter, but this disconnects us from the intelligence within it.

Bald, hunched, and moustachioed, the old man shuffled along the platform, his wife and the porters following. Max Planck, the father of quantum physics, had arrived in Florence to speak at a conference. He hadn't slept much and was longing for his hotel room, but at least it was warmer on the South side of the Alps.

Earlier in the year, enemy bombers had destroyed their flat in Berlin, together with many of his precious papers: the results of a lifetime's dedication to science. War had taken many people he'd known, including his eldest son, killed in the trenches.

He'd known others lost to the cruelty of the current regime and had even tried to argue face to face with Hitler for a change of policy towards the Jews. Later on, he would lose his second son, executed after a failed attempt on Hitler's life. But what kept him going was the hope that science would give humanity enough understanding to mature.

And he was fascinated by the mysteries of matter and consciousness. In a few days he would speak about this in his presentation:

Having studied the atom, I am telling you that there is no matter as such. All matter arises and persists only due to a force

that causes the atomic particles to vibrate, holding them together
in the tiniest of solar systems: the atom. We must assume behind
this force the existence of a conscious and intelligent mind.
This mind is the matrix of all matter. [17]

Planck's insight that behind matter there is conscious intelligence challenges the orthodox assumption. It seems obvious that matter is "dead." How could a great scientist like Max Planck dispute that?

Matter is a mystery. It seems solid, but quantum physicists like Planck tell us it has far more space than particles. We experience it as solid because of our perspective. Matter feels dense, but Einstein's theory of special relativity explains that matter and energy are interchangeable. Matter comes into form when light beams collide. This is an awesome mystery, and opening to it brings us into a relationship of respect with it.

According to many Indigenous elders, including my teachers, all energy has consciousness. Both in the seen and unseen, the whole Universe is humming with energy-consciousness. It is an eternal cosmic dance in which all things are interrelated. All things influence each other. All forms in this dance of energy—stars, planets, plants, animals, humans, the weather and so on—emerge from the formless, and all forms are temporary. But behind form is the formless; behind the temporary is the timeless.

For me, the concept that all energy has consciousness is a working perspective that brings a more vital and respectful relationship with the Self and life. For much of my adult life, I looked at matter as inanimate, but I have worked to overcome this conditioning of "dead-matter thinking." Opening to the possibility that all energy has consciousness brings us into a bigger relationship with life—more awake, aware, and in awe of the mystery that touches us in each moment. I become more physically present and able to respect both the diversity of phenomena and the unity of consciousness within and behind them.

The minerals of this earth are in a dynamic living relationship with Earth's other offspring such as fungi, plants, and animals. All these forms are emanations of spirit as light and are part of the evolutionary unfolding of life on Earth. Mineral evolution takes place through cosmic forces but on Earth there is increasing complexity of mineral species because of interaction with plants and animals. Limestone is an example of this growing diversity in that it is formed partly by tiny sea creatures processing calcium carbonate.

"Sacred" means "holy", and "holy' has to do with wholeness. When we create ceremony we hold a sacred space in which to connect with wholeness, and connecting with wholeness is the essential meaning of healing. Sacred space means honouring the living relationship with our Earth and with the healing power within, and a ceremony enables us to access deeper parts of our consciousness such as our healing energy and intuition.

Respect for the external reflects respect for the internal. Respect for the planet means respect for the person. Learning to honour the personal and the planetary go together. To "desecrate" literally means to "take away the sacredness," and our desecration of nature has been caused in part by "dead-matter thinking." We need to find a new reverence for the material world. As one of my teachers put it: "Even trash is sacred."

The minerals of this earth are in a dynamic living relationship with Earth's other offspring such as fungi, plants, and animals. All these forms are emanations of spirit as light and are part of the evolutionary unfolding of life on Earth. Mineral evolution takes place through cosmic forces but on Earth there is increasing complexity of mineral species because of interaction with plants and animals. Limestone is an example of this growing diversity in that it is formed partly by tiny sea creatures processing calcium carbonate.

In the Medicine lineage I have followed, we often sit together in a Medicine Wheel. There is a protocol to speak the words "All my relations" as we enter or leave the Medicine Wheel. This is a reminder that everything is related; all of life is in relationship; and all things come from the matrix, the quantum field, the teeming womb of life. So speaking these words awakens respect and even reverence for the mystery of consciousness as we come in or out of the Wheel.

There is a sense of respect for the mystery of matter in the subterranean soil of language. The word *matrix* means "womb" in Latin and has common roots with "matter" and "mother." Like the Sanskrit *matar*, meaning "mother," they come from a common linguistic ancestor: Indo-European. Our own ancestors may have sensed that this world of form, Mother Earth, is a womb for our spirit. Behind form, the formless gives birth to us and to this womb in which we live and grow. Beneath the surface appearance of solidity, subtle levels of consciousness are at play.

Mother Earth is a being of vast consciousness. Like all of creation, she has masculine as well as feminine aspects. She does not belong to us; we belong to her. We are her expressions. She has given birth to countless offspring, and we are part of her. She is in us, and we in her. She is sacred; we are sacred.

What does "to respect" really mean? One understanding is "to see beyond the surface." When we hold the lens of "all energy has consciousness," we see beyond the surface; we see the sacred. When we see the sacred, we call it forward in ourselves and others. So this lens—"all energy has consciousness"—evokes respect for the sacred. It heightens consciousness.

Healing our relationship with the earth is essential for our own healing. We can begin to do so by rediscovering reverence for the spirit in matter. This heightening of consciousness means respect for the earth and for our bodies, respect for ourselves and for each other. It means putting care of Mother Earth at the heart of politics and making peace between economy and ecology. And it means bringing ourselves into balance.

PRACTICE: Body Meditation

This is a practice to create sacred space in which to access our healing, intuition, and wisdom. We will use our own body as an object of meditation and access the alive-consciousness in matter by putting attention on the vitality within the body.

Sit with your spine erect. Take four slow, deep breaths, inhaling through the nose and out through the mouth. As you breathe out, allow your jaw to relax and any tension around your forehead and eyes to melt. Notice the contact of your body with your seat and ground. Notice gravity holding you to the earth. As your presence deepens, notice the feeling inside your feet—the bones, muscles, and sinews. Be with the inner aliveness. Gradually let this awareness spread into your ankles and lower legs, knees, and thighs; now into your buttocks, genitals, and hips. Savour the sense of vital life-energy in your body. Gradually expand your awareness up the spine—abdomen . . . chest and shoulders . . . down the arms and into the hands . . . up into the neck, face, and head.

Allow your attention to rest in the whole physical body. Feel it as a single energy field.

Be in deep communion with the body. Contemplate its miracle: the numberless cells sustaining life, the complex beauty of interrelated systems working together, the organs that generate the ineffable richness of our life experience—senses, voice, brain, heart, emotions, sex, and so on. This form of matter emerges from Mother Earth, an expression of the sun. Open to this mystery. Sense the vital force that animates this matter.

Contemplation means letting go of heady thought. It is a state of presence in which we connect with all life and sense the Universe within. This is the source of deep wisdom that's in all of us. Remain in this state as long as you wish.

The Dynamic Dance
of Opposites

What would life be like if we saw ourselves as sacred, or everything as sacred? What would our relationship with Earth be like? How would we treat other people? How would we treat ourselves? Honouring the sacredness of all life would make a radical difference to all our relationships. It would mean relating to every part of our Self with an attitude of deep caring. It would strengthen our healing, resilience, and sustainability, because an attitude of self-care is a vital ingredient for these qualities. Respecting the Self as a sacred being is a foundation on this leg of our journey.

The traditions of Earth Wisdom evolved among people who lived in close relationship with Earth. They honoured her as a sacred being. They studied her ways: her cycles, tides, weather patterns, animals, and plant and mineral expressions. They were conscious that she provides all that we need to sustain our lives and can teach us many things. One of them is balance.

There is a dynamic balance in nature. Flowers open in sunlight and close in the darkness. Animals move between being asleep and awake. The breath comes in, the breath goes out. The heart pulses between diastole and systole. And our consciousness ebbs and flows with serotonin and melatonin, the neurotransmitters of sun and moon. All life forms have the twin balancing energies of feminine and masculine. One is yielding and receptive, the other is penetrating and changing. Realizing that we have both energies in us enhances our ability to nurture ourselves.

But how can we care for this dynamic balance?

I remember one Saturday just before Christmas when I was shopping with my family. Everyone was excited, and I felt an echo of childhood thrill about the coming holidays, too. But I'd been busy for a long time, and my wife and I still had much to do. We felt pressured.

We went to an indoor market of crowds and cafes, stalls, bustle, and busyness. Some folky musicians were playing "Silent Night" on bass, violin, and accordion, but no one seemed to be listening. Everyone was fighting to get through, hunting for gifts, and the atmosphere was frantic and frenetic. I felt frazzled.

Noticing pressure boiling up, I went outside for air. Taking a deep breath and looking down at the outdoor market, I took in the whole scene with my peripheral vision—colours, movement, sounds, and smells. I watched birds and clouds overhead. I let go of overwhelm, and it set my spirit free again. My physical tightness uncoiled, thought-waves smoothened and aura expanded. I reconnected with being. I wondered why our modern culture gets so busy in the depths of winter when the rest of nature is fast asleep. How had we become so out of balance with ourselves and with nature?

Living close to the planet, our ancestors honoured the cycle of the year in regular ceremonies. This renewed their relationship with life and helped them care for inner balance. At the equinoxes, they celebrated the balance of night and day, and at the solstices the dance between light and dark. They would salute the quickening of new life in spring, dance to honour the summer sun, and give thanks for the harvest in autumn.

But in winter, when the Earth is covered by a blanket of leaves or snow, when the energy of trees sinks back to their roots, when the seeds of new growth lie dormant in the dark soil, when the animals retreat to their burrows, when even the bear goes into her cave to dream, they would go into silence and darkness to allow the void of all potential to renew their dreaming. It helped them maintain the balance of being and becoming.

In our current mainstream, it is easy to forget about being and only focus on becoming. We may assume that it is "good" to be busy all the time. Our thinking becomes preoccupied with doing, and we neglect our inner state. We become engrossed with getting: getting things, getting places, or getting better. We then get overwhelmed and imbalanced. But it need only take a tenth of a second to reconnect with being—by putting attention on our breath, inner body, or sense-perceptions.

Being present is one aspect of self-respect and self-care. As we saw in the chapter on the Southeast, presence gives us awareness of our current condition. When we look within, we can perceive what our spirit, emotion, body, and heart-mind need for wholeness and balance. With this awareness, we activate the innate healing of the west. We nurture ourselves and strengthen our resilience. We see what we need to teach ourselves in order to sustain a balanced life.

Sometimes the way to strengthen ourselves is to do more—to challenge ourselves more, for example, or to exercise more. At other times we need to go into the cave and regenerate our energy through rest. It has been said that in our current culture we spend less time asleep than earlier generations—because of artificial lighting and our urge to do and get. But consider this story:

> *Once there was a king. One day he looked out of the window of his palace at the city below and the surrounding countryside. Watching his people go about their business and seeing them toil to make their living, the king thought: I wonder how I could help them? What would be the best policy, the best thing I could do to help them?*
>
> *So he sent for his counsellor. And when his counsellor arrived, the king asked him: "What is the best thing I could do to help my people?"*
>
> *And the counsellor replied: "Great King, the best way you can help your people is to sleep as much as you can. The less you interfere the better."*

Sometimes it helps more to do less. We need the East energy of self-expression and creativity, but we need to balance it with the West energy of inwardness and introspection. Introspection opens the door to intuition so that we understand how to care for ourselves and come back into balance.

When our energy is balanced, we give balanced energy to the world. So caring for ourselves is not a selfish indulgence; it is vital for our world. There is much to do to restore the collective consciousness to balance, but when we bring ourselves into balance we help restore the collective balance. And when we are in balance, we have no need to compensate by overconsuming Earth's resources or abusing our Self or others.

In the next section, we'll explore the balance of the four elements in and around us, and how our relationship with them enhances our innate healing power.

PRACTICE: Introspection

First, create a safe and sacred space in which to look within. Make it nurturing and beautiful. Arrange to not be interrupted; put phones on silent or off the hook. You may like to go alone into nature.

Open the practice with a ritual gesture of leaving behind everyday activity and ordinary thinking. This could be ritual washing of hands, feet, and face, for example.

Now take four deep breaths to help your consciousness to drop an octave or two. As you inhale, direct the energy into the point just below the navel, the womb or will centre. And let the exhale carry away stress or tension.

Look within with a caring, benevolent attitude. Without judgement, notice if anything is out of balance. This is not about puzzling things out with your brain-mind. Let the deeper wisdom come to the surface through intuition.

You can practise introspection about balance. You may like to speak your questions aloud, then allow insights to come: "What is needed for wholeness and balance?" "How can I take better care of myself and my world?" "How can I maintain the various relationships of my life?"

Introspection is particularly needed when something has impacted you. It could have been something unfamiliar or a situation similar to one you've been in before.

See this as an opportunity to learn something and to empower yourself. Hold questions such as these: "What pattern am I repeating?" "How did I help create this?" "What am I to learn from this?" "What signals did I miss?" "What might I do differently next time?"

Introspection enables us to reap the full harvest of learning from a situation. It helps us see what we need, to return to balance before going back into action.

The Medicine of the
Four Elements

As we become conscious of the spirit within matter, let us deepen our relationship with its four primary expressions: earth, air, fire, and water. Becoming intimate with them deepens our natural healing power.

In the winter of 1847, a young man was walking by the River Danube, coughing up blood. Coughing, coughing, coughing—with each bout he could feel his life force ebbing away. He was suffering the same illness that consumed the lives of many of his contemporaries— the Brontes, Balzac, Keats, Kafka, Chopin, and Chekhov among them. It seemed he was going the same way.

There was no vaccine, no known cure for "consumption," as tuberculosis was then known. But Sebastian Kneipp had come across a little book that described the healing power of water. It suggested immersing yourself, and with nothing left to lose, he decided to give it a try.

It was freezing cold, but he jumped in the river. After a minute or two in the shocking waters, he hurried back to his room to warm up. The blood came rushing from the core to his skin, and he actually felt a little better, certainly no worse. He decided to make this water treatment his medicine, and throughout that winter he jumped in the Danube several times a week—and survived.

Bathing in cold water may benefit various health conditions, from cardio-vascular to depression. It stimulates a response from the natural healing power in all of us, the force that keeps us alive. Kneipp lived a further 50 years.

Inspired by his own healing, Kneipp began to offer water treatments to many others, including the pope of the time, Leo XIII, and Archduke Franz Ferdinand (who was later shot at Sarajevo). Apart from hydrotherapy, Kneipp prescribed other natural medicine, such as fresh air, sunshine, and exercise. No one had to pay for these remedies, and they were available to everyone. Kneipp went on to become one of the most famous people in Germany.

In many times and places healers have worked with the power of nature. Hippocrates, Empedocles, Galen, and Charaka, the father of Ayurvedic medicine, all encouraged patients to relate with the four elements.

Around the same time as Kneipp, Florence Nightingale, one of the most famous healers in Britain, also understood that fresh air and sunlight are healing energies. She noticed that wounded soldiers were more likely to survive if left outside on the battlefield than taken into a field hospital, so she designed hospitals to encourage airflow and rays of sunlight. "Never be afraid of open windows," she wrote.

Mainstream medicine has changed greatly since then. The rise of antibiotics eclipsed the use of those healing elements, but now we face a crisis brought on by overuse of them. Perhaps mainstream medicine will rediscover the healing benefits of the elements again.

It may be interesting to look for the mechanism by which the elements heal—the stimulus to blood flow of cold water, for example, or increased vitamin D from sunlight, or fresh air killing off microbes. But it's a mistake to reduce the elements to simple physiology. They are spirit, and there is something deeper and more mysterious about them.

Earth Medicine is not a system of healthcare, but it cares about health. The root of the word "health" is the old Anglo-Saxon *haelu*, which had the sense of life force, good fortune, prosperity, and spiritual blessing. It also gives us the words "holy," "holistic," and "wholeness." We need to see the Self as "holy," our approach to health needs to be "holistic," and we need to seek our "wholeness." This we can do through our relationship with earth, air, fire, and water.

We too have four elements, four aspects of the Self: spirit, mind, emotion, and body. These four are interrelated; what affects one affects all, and our health and wholeness depend on the balance of all four.

How does our relationship with the four elements feed the health and balance of these four aspects of Self? The elements are in everything around us, dancing together in many forms and combinations. They are in us, in our breath and bone, in our fluidity, and in the mitochondria that fire our energy. They exist in the seen and unseen, and when we direct our thought-power to them, they respond to it. But let's now consider these essential life forces more deeply.

First let's think about fire. What powers the Universe? In the galaxies of luminosity spread across the darkness of space, cosmic fire; in the nuclear fusion at the heart of our sun, elemental fire; in magma under the earth's skin, volcanic fire; in the growing leaves of fruits and flowers, the fire of photosynthesis; and in the micro-furnaces of our cells, the chemical fire of our life force.

Fire gives life. But how well do we tend our fire? If our thoughts, words, and deeds are fuel, which ones keep it bright and which dampen it? What sparks our passion and purpose? What does our spirit cry out for? And how can we keep our fire from raging out of control? How do we keep it lively yet safe?

Fire needs a container; earth provides the hearth. Earth bears life in many forms. Her mineral substance gives us our bones, our structure. The minerals come from the light of creation and are evolving into diverse forms—rocks, sands, and gravels, crystals and gemstones, ores and metals. Earth substance provides us the forms by which we live—not only our bodies but also our food, clothes, and shelter. And all the tools that humans have ever wielded, from stone axes to silicon chips, have come from the earth.

How well do we care for the structures that sustain us? What do we need to strengthen in our body, mind, emotion, and spirit? What does our body need for health? Are we quiet enough to hear its voice or even the voice of Earth herself?

Now consider water. We may take it for granted—it's just H_2O, isn't it? But when we drink or run a tap, we connect with all water, because all water is connected—waves and holy wells, rains and rivers, clouds and cascades, steam, snow, sleet, slush, sea-spume, and saline solution. Yet it's also an enigma. Liquid, solid, or gas—it is energy-consciousness expressing itself in an infinite diversity of crystal light. The ocean is a principal energy field on this blue planet, and when feelings run in saltwater on our cheeks, it is the power of ocean flowing through us.

How can we care for water, for the aquatic systems in and around us and for the emotional part of our mind? How can this power of fluidity help us move forward with trust? Can we open to our inner currents and tides of feeling and allow them to inform us without being flooded?

And there is the invisible power of air, the wind that blows ceaselessly around our planet, from arctic blast to the mildest zephyr, oxygenating blood and brain, infusing heart-mind and organs with pranic life force. The blueness of sky is balm for our eyes and soul, and in each moment of our breathing life, we draw from this azure veil—Earth's aura.

Many schools of consciousness work with the breath, including yoga, rebirthing, and martial arts. How can breath—sky, air—be our ally in our journey of growing consciousness? And how does it inform our heart-mind of what we need to do next? Holding these questions in communion with the elements deepens our relationship with their essence, the beauty behind them.

Once, my teacher recommended that I talk to the elements about my self-doubt. I spent several hours on the shore, listening to the sound of surf, feeling sand as soft as silk, receiving the blessing of sun and cloud. It began the healing of my old sense of isolation and lack of confidence. And the more I give the power of attention to my kinship with the elements, the more I identify not as separate but as an expression of life with their power flowing through me.

We are here to learn from these primary expressions of life force. Awakening our relationship with fire, earth, air, and water and balancing the inner elements of spirit, body, mind, and emotion are interrelated.

When we realize the balance in nature, we realize the balance in ourselves. And by developing our relationship with the elements, we evolve our healing intelligence.

PRACTICE: Healing with the Four Elements

The primordial power of the four elements is strong in the wild. Here, we connect with spirit, for example, by dancing round a bonfire or gazing at stars. We can step into the sea or river and let water cleanse our emotion. We may need to strengthen our body by walking in the mountains or sitting on sand. And we can breathe deep and let wind clear and vitalize our consciousness.

We can also drop into deep communion indoors with symbolic representations, such as a candle, a bowl of water, rocks, and feathers.

Either way, we come into conscious relationship by directing attention to them. We can ask them directly for teaching and healing, then open to their subtle responses.

We can also balance the human elements by holding questions, not working out answers with the brain but allowing responses to emerge. As well as the questions mentioned in the previous section, we can hold these:

"How is my spirit fire?"

"What do I need to keep it bright?"

"How are my feelings?"

"How can I deepen my trust in myself?"

"What's needed to heal and strengthen in my body?"

"Can I access courage and clarity?"

"Are there any blockages to the natural balance of these human elements, and if so, how can I clear them?"

These are ways to receive the elemental blessing and celebrate the gift of life.

Death Is an Ally

I have a memory from when I was aged 10: I was cycling to a playing field to meet friends. I had a red bicycle and used to imagine I was a knight on my trusty steed. But on this occasion, my quest had turned existential: I was wondering if life continued after death, or not.

The enigma of death confronts all mortals. What happens when we die? What is it that animates us in life, and where does it go, if anywhere? What happened to the people we knew who have died? How did they change from breathing beings into lifeless corpses? Does life have meaning? Or is it but a walking shadow, a brief candle?

There are many ways to deal with these questions. One way is to avoid them altogether, but actively facing the reality of death brings us into more wholeness. Many people find accepting our own mortality reduces anxiety and increases appreciation of the present moment. And whatever our beliefs about it, how we relate to death makes a difference to how we experience life.

As I cycled along the lane, it came to me that I didn't have much to worry about. If there was life after death I would carry on, and if there wasn't, I wouldn't be around to regret it. That settled it, at least for a while, and I was free to play.

Since then, I've explored the mystery of death in different ways. What I have to write here is based on this inquiry and informed by understandings from Medicine and other traditions.

A hundred years ago, sex was taboo in polite society; now the taboo is death. This avoidance causes imbalance. Mainstream culture focuses on the material and not on the unseen. Besides, many of us feel awkward about grief. We don't want death to spoil the party. It is healthy to bring this skeleton out of the closet. Whoever we are, death is waiting for us somewhere—perhaps playing on a phone in some coffee shop or in a queue at the airport. Accepting that we are going to meet death at some unknown time can heighten our appreciation of life; instead of being our foe, death can become an ally in the battle to awaken consciousness.

Being aware of our mortality and of our closeness to the light of eternity helps us live in the present more vividly. Life only takes place here in the present moment. This awareness frees us. It helps us be closer to our essence. We sense the timeless behind the temporary. We accept that one day we'll walk through the door; as far as possible, we let go of fearing it. And when we notice we're caught up in petty concerns or worries, we can step back to remember our deeper purpose. Let's be true to our dreams. Let's reach for our greatness and nobility.

I assume that if you're reading these words, you're still alive in the physical world of form. It has been said that the state we go into after death is similar to our dreams at night. When we're awake, we perceive the solidity of the world around us, but we can be asleep in the same place and perceive an entirely different reality, one that is equally real to our dreaming self. This afternoon, my body was asleep here in the physical realm, but "I" dreamed I was somewhere else. There, I met my dead father and gave him a hug.

In some shamanic cultures, it has been said that the veil between this world and that of the dead is as thin as a sheet of paper. Most of the time we, the living, don't look through the veil because our attention is absorbed by the physical world, but in some states—physical or emotional extremes, for example—we may see through and again experience those we've known who have died.

Some years ago, I went to northern New Mexico to take part in a ceremonial dance, the Sun-Moon Dance. A group of us set up a circular space in the high desert with a tree at the centre. We danced back and forth to the tree for several days without food and water. Our intention was to go into a visionary state. Dancing and dry fasting in the high desert during a heat wave, part of you suffers. As the dance goes on, you start to walk out on the thin line between life and death, into a kind of deathbed state of consciousness, a little like a rehearsal for death itself. I noticed that as I went beyond exhaustion, my body felt frailer, but another part of me started feeling strong and energized.

I started to see people who weren't in the physical world of form. They were "with us," but part of me had difficulty with this. I had been educated to be rational and work with empirical evidence—to dismiss anything that didn't fit in with that consensus reality. But these people knew they were real. They were wearing ribbons and feathers and happily dancing along with me. And by the end of my dance I felt the support of a tribal grandmother, even as, in the physical dimension, people were carrying me out and dripping water into my mouth.

A few weeks after my father died, I wanted to see if I could make contact with him. I went into a dreamy state and found a house, the front of which was an ordinary façade while the rear was underground, extending back into a hillside. Inside the house, I met my father and told him we hadn't been able to do anything with his books—he'd said he wanted them to go to his old university, but they didn't want them.

"Oh, don't worry," he said, showing me a vast library. "I've all the books you could ever want to read."

Death is not the opposite of life; it's the opposite of birth. Birth and death are doorways through which we pass on the great circle of learning. Death supports life; the death of plants and animals gives us the food that sustains us. We live because others die; we take their energy when we eat; we transform their life force and pass it on in new expressions of energy. It's one circle.

The circle has twin forces: one of growth and one of decay. But when things are in decay, they are feeding those that grow. Look at a mature tree. Part of it is growing by feeding on sunlight, soil, air, and water, and another part is decaying to feed new forms of growth.

The cells of our bodies also live and die; when they die, new ones grow. If some of them stop dying and start multiplying, that condition may cause us to die. Then those cells, too, will die, and this body that has given us life will break down and feed life in new ways. Our form will return to the earth from which, in a sense, we borrowed it. But as our form dissolves, if we allow ourselves, we open to the light we have always been.

Of course, grief can feel excruciating when someone close dies. We lose their physical presence, and our heart feels like it is breaking. But grief may break us open to see what's truly important to us. It can help us be less attached to what's not important. Grief breaks the heart open to experience each precious moment more vividly. And with our hearts cracked open, we release those who are precious to us with love.

If I were to speak to that boy on a bicycle now, what would I say? I'd probably thank him for asking those questions and encourage him to keep asking them. And I might agree with him: nothing to worry about, on to play in the next field.

PRACTICE: Making Death an Ally

Come into a state of contemplation. Take a few slow, deep breaths, releasing any concerns as you breathe out—let Mother Earth have them for now. Feel the vitality in your body. Notice your skeleton.

This body sustains you in life, but it will return to the earth in death. Remember the light of eternity that surrounds you. Use the awareness of mortality to expand your perspective. Savour the preciousness of each moment.

Death is an opportunity for transformation and growth. Knowing that the time of death is uncertain, contemplate these questions:

What preparation do you need to make for death?
Are there any old friends you'd like to get in touch with?
What unfinished business do you need to complete?
What do you need to forgive in yourself or others?
How can you take more Self-responsibility?

What fears do you need to work through, and what do you need to heal?

What do you need to accept in yourself?

Knowing that at some point you will die, how do you want to live? What practices do you want to take up?

How can you expand your consciousness?

How can you be more open to learning from the Infinite Self?

Do you have time for petty thoughts?

Accepting the inevitability of our death enables us to live with more wholeness. Make a note of any action you choose to take as a result of this contemplation.

All Energy Has Consciousness

6

Northwest: Dreaming

 Moving clockwise around the Medicine Wheel we have opened the creative, perceptual, emotional, intentional, and healing consciousness. Here in the Northwest, we enter the realm of dreaming. This is our power to influence the future through collaboration with the Universe.

The energy centre of the Northwest is the body-mind. The body-mind is a marvel of interconnectedness and cooperation among cells, organs, and systems—bone, blood and breath, lymph, lungs and liver, nervous, digestive, endocrine, and so on. This sensitive web is a vast field of subtle intelligence. It shows its genius in the gaps between ordinary thought, for example, in our innate sense of timing and intuitive knowing. It sends and receives messages from the Universe. But much of its communication is subconscious or unconscious.

While we're awake, we're often unconscious of the body-mind because our attention is on the outer world. When we close our eyes and go inward, we're more receptive to it. During sleep, the body-mind releases information in night dreams. We can learn better recall of night dreams and become conscious in them (lucid dreaming). But asleep or awake, dreaming is going on all the time.

A way to access the power of dreaming is through its complementary opposite in the Southeast: presence. By stilling the surface waters of our thought, we gain access to the oceanic depths of our dreaming mind. We also expand awareness of our thoughts, feelings, words, and actions and how they are influencing the future. This enables us to be more conscious dreamers.

Mainstream culture marginalizes the body-mind and dreaming.

A dominant cultural belief claims that "consciousness" is the same as ordinary thinking, but this limits our sense of human consciousness and potential. Giving attention to night dreams, we expand to a vaster sense of Self and the potential of our relationship with the Mystery.

If we studied our dreams, each of us could write a book about dreaming: it's a vast subject. **Night Dreaming** offers ways to open this field.

In the Northwest is the principle of interrelatedness and the law of cycles. Everything in our Universe is interrelated, and energy moves in cycles. Some cycles are obvious: day and night, for example, or the change of seasons as Earth dances around the sun. Others are not easy to observe—the 26,000-year precession of the equinoxes or the life cycles of stars and spiral movements of galaxies across time and space.

Our body is not separate from the light of Spirit that permeates all things in the Universe. Like stars and planets, it is a vibration of the Divine. It has many cycles—heartbeat and pulse, for example; in-breath and out-breath; and the cycle of sleep and awake. It has rhythm and timing. Its intelligence is intuitive and predictive, not rational or deductive. It picks up information beyond the brain-mind. It has a kind of genius to it, a sensitivity to subtle impressions.

Since everything in our Universe is interrelated, every cause leads to effects. This is the Law of Sequence. Everything we do leads to an effect, even actions that seem insignificant. Clouds gather; rain falls and rivers flow. We drink; later we need to urinate. What we do now affects what is to come. How we think and speak in this moment causes effects later on. We co-create the future with the dreaming Universe. Our thoughts, words, and actions shape it. Becoming conscious of this principle of co-creation is vital in transforming the global situation.

The Pebble and the Paddling Pool goes into this power and the Law of Cause and Effect.

Dreams relate to many levels of our consciousness. In day-to-day waking consciousness, our attention is often wholly taken up by our individuality, but we humans are also a collective field. This collective consciousness is a river of wisdom flowing with the experience of all humans who have lived, are living, and will live. We can open ourselves to this wisdom, and may sometimes receive it in "great dreams" that relate to more than our individual consciousness. **The Tower and the Birds** is an example of this kind of dream.

This power of dreaming includes our ability to see the patterns and cycles that are coming towards us through the web of interrelationship. We can direct our attention to the "dreaming" that takes place in waking life in order to see and intuit signs. **Whispers of the Oracle** is about this divinatory state of consciousness.

Night Dreaming

When we sleep we dream. A quarter of people say they don't remember dreams, but all of us have them. Research suggests that all mammals dream; opossums and armadillos are especially prolific dreamers. From the moment of our conception to that of our last perception, we are dreamers. We dream in beds and bunks, cots and cradles, under blankets and skins, on hay and in hammocks. Babies spend most of their time dreaming, and on average adults have three to five dreams a night—some have seven. Over a typical lifetime, we spend about six years dreaming. And even when we move off from our deathbed, we dream.

I recall a dream I had at the age of 18. I was being pursued by some nasty Nazis. In the dream, I am running along a maze of corridors in a building similar to my school. They are coming to get me, and nothing I do can shake them off. At last, I find a window that I can open. I climb out and run from the building. But they know where I am and follow me across the lawn. I get a little ahead and leave the path to hide in some bushes. Perhaps they'll go past. But when they come level, they sense me and turn after me again. And I wake up.

I felt fear in the dream, and it coloured my mood the next morning. It had been so vivid and puzzling that I went to the library and looked up books on dreams. As I did so, some words of a Bob Marley song floated up from the subconscious: "You're running, and you're running, and you're running away, but you can't run away from your Self."

They gave me a hunch about the dream's message. I had recently left the labyrinth of life at school, where external authorities had pursued me. Now I needed to find my own self-authority and meet aspects of the

Self that I hadn't identified with. By this point in my life, I'd decided I was an atheist. I had been culturally conditioned to dismiss dreams and non-rational states of consciousness. I saw myself as limited and separate, an isolated identity in a world of dead matter, and I lent little credence to anything other than the surface appearance of things.

This paradigm is pervasive, but our true identity is far grander than this. Dreaming opens us to our depths and heights. Our nightly voyages on the dark ocean of dreams are vital to our wellbeing, and we marginalize them to our cost.

That dream was a signpost on my path. It reignited my interest in psyche and spirit, and I began to keep a notebook by my bed to record dreams. It wasn't my last dream of being chased, but I gradually trained myself to turn and face anything that came after me in dreams. In a later dream, I was chased by Thai dragons, but when I turned to look at them, they stopped.

I learned this from reading about the Senoi, a tribe of hunter-gatherers in Malaysia. The book suggested that the Senoi were a powerful dreaming culture. It said that they didn't teach children to dismiss nightmares as "just a dream" but to confront any dangers or enemies in dreams.[18] If a child dreamed of being attacked by a tiger, for example, they learned to fight dream tigers or call on friends to help them. They learned to make friends with dream characters and to honour dream gifts by expressing them creatively. According to the book, these teachings on the art of dreaming enabled the Senoi to create a healthy and harmonious society.

Night dreams are beyond reason, and their purpose cannot be completely defined. They are an education for the inner Self and call us to introspect. They teach us through symbols and lead us to develop intuition; they offer new perspectives and reflections on things we haven't seen before; they work out energies we haven't digested while awake; they bring healing and learning; and they prepare us to meet what is coming.

If the psyche were like a house, our personal Self might be the ground floor. We probably spend much of our waking time there; perhaps in the office of reason and analysis. But there are many rooms to explore on the floors above and below; dreams show us the stairs. They connect us with our totality. They may show us where we need to alter the structure or build an extension. And sometimes they reveal artefacts buried in the deep strata of consciousness.

Reason and analysis are useful in many ways, but they are not breakthrough states of consciousness. Breakthroughs often come from dreams of the night or day. Behind the visible world of manifestation is the unseen realm of dreaming, and when we yield to it, we allow the muses to inspire us.

For example, the German chemist August Kekulé had been trying to work out the shape of the benzene molecule before he entered a dream state and dreamed of a snake swallowing its own tail. This ancient symbol, the "ouroboros," inspired his breakthrough in chemistry.

Another example is the invention of the sewing machine. Elias Howe had been working on the design of a machine to make sewing easier. He then dreamed of being chased, caught, and cooked by cannibals. As he tried to get out of their cooking pot, they repeatedly stabbed him to keep him in, and he noticed that each of their spears had a hole in the tip. When he woke up with this image, he realized the breakthrough. He knew how to arrange the hole in the needle to make the sewing machine work.

A good way to work with the meaning of dream symbols is to feel the images in our body. Our body-mind gives us access to intuition. By directing attention to how our body feels when we think of a dream image, we intuit its meaning. We can let the feeling move us, draw or enact it, or write a description. Opening to the subtle levels of dreams enables their messages to unfold.

Where do dreams come from? They've been variously put down to Morpheus, Queen Mab, or Roald Dahl's BFG, but whatever their origin, they are expressions of the Mystery. Our body-mind is a huge field of intelligence made of light, an interconnected web of subtle energies that receives impressions from the Universe. It translates this information and expresses it as messages to our subconscious and unconscious mind. This is communication from the Infinite to the personal.

This communication is happening all the time, but in ordinary waking states, we are not aware of it. When we're asleep, the body-mind expresses these messages as dreams. If we recall them, we can open the intuition and allow their symbolic content to support our evolution.

We can strengthen our access to the dreamtime while we're awake. One way is by daydreaming and taking brief dips into the hypnagogic borderlands of sleep. Another is to suspend ordinary thinking, open to the subtle levels of experience, and follow the dreaming muse. These ways give us access to the fecund inspiration of this rich realm.

The night dream is different from waking life, but it is not an entirely separate reality. By using the powers of attention and intention, we build a bridge between these two sides of our Self so that they support each other. We can intend to connect with our sleeping Self and ask our dreams for insight and healing. Or we can take inspiration from our dream gifts and re-enact them, or create something in the physical realm to mirror them. Thus we bring our two sides into closer alignment, and by bridging them, we become more intimate with magic, marvels, and the miraculous.

PRACTICE: Bridging the Day Dream and Night Dream

Increase communication between your waking and sleeping selves by giving attention to bridging the gap between them. The most potent time to do this is in the twilight as you cross between them, just before or after sleep.

Before going to sleep, focus your dreaming intention. The focus could be to increase dream recall or to dream about a particular issue by asking for healing and insight about it. A way to intend to lucid-dream is by spending five minutes looking at your hands while actively commanding yourself: "Tonight when I dream, I will find my hands and realize that I am dreaming." Carry this command as far as possible into sleep. Then find your hands while dreaming and give the command: "More lucidity now!"

You can use symbols to amplify your intention by placing symbolic objects near your bed. For example, a bowl or other receptacle could symbolize your receptivity if you are calling for inspiration or answers to a question. Keep a notebook and pen nearby to record notes or pictures of your dreams.

In these ways you are directing the attention of your waking Self to remember your sleeping Self. If you become conscious that you are dreaming, you can then encourage your sleeping self to remember your waking self.

To increase recall, emerge from sleep gently. Let your dream experiences crystallize in memory by staying still as your dreaming body re-enters your physical body. If you recall a snippet, ask what happened before it; it is possible to retrieve whole dreams by drawing them out like this. Express appreciation for the dreams you've received, even if you don't recall them consciously. Interpret any snippets or whole dreams in the light of the intention you set.

Yield to the dream. Introspect the most numinous or impactful symbols by "becoming" them in your imagination. What do they remind you of? Draw them, speak from them, enact them, conjure with them. Allow your intuitive insight to unfold in its own way.

The Pebble and the Paddling Pool

Having touched on the huge subject of night-dreaming, let us now consider how we shape the future through the law of cause and effect.

Dreaming does not only take place at night; we're dreaming all the time. What we call reality is a dream-field in which we are dreaming and being dreamed. We sow the dream-field with our thoughts, words, and deeds; these seeds are nurtured in the dark soil of Universal energy-consciousness, and their fruit emerges in consequence. What we experience is co-created with the rest of the Universe.

We live in a co-creative Universe. When we say "I am dreaming, it means that I am affecting the energy in and around me. All of my conscious-ness—images, feelings, and utterances—is rippling out and causing effects in the rest of the Universe. I influence what happens but can't control the outcome, because countless other things are also influencing it. All things in the Universe are "dreaming;" we are creating together.

Life is always offering us challenges to help us grow strong. The consciousness with which we respond to them is a primary influence on how they turn out. Whatever action we choose, how we feel and think is of major importance. We can think of ourselves as victims or we can see our challenges as opportunities to empower ourselves and grow in wisdom. When we see that all things are interrelated in this mysterious, co-creative Universe we understand that we are both the dreamers and the dreamed. This puts us in the centre of our circle.

I once spoke about this to a group of schoolchildren while we were standing around a paddling pool. I asked them to imagine that the still water represented the energy within and all around us. Then I handed out pebbles to represent our thoughts, words, and actions and said: "Let's see what effect they have on this field of energy."

We threw our pebbles in and watched the ripples emanating outwards, crossing and interacting with each other. One of the children remarked: "It's like when you throw a coin in a wishing well!"

"Exactly," I said. "Everything we think, say, and do ripples out into the energy field, but not all our thoughts come true, not in the way we expect. And it's partly because everything else is making wishes too."

I'd gone into the primary school my daughter attended—Park School in Devon, England—and was running a project called The Children's Fire. Working with the teachers, our intention was to bring self-knowledge teachings and tools to children. Could we plant seeds to help the next generation know themselves better? Could we help them understand that they're never separate from life and are always affecting things around them?

That day standing around the paddling pool, several of the class and their teacher were away in London. They were in a competition to win a new classroom the school needed badly. The rules were that the class had to design the classroom, and in that very moment the absent children might have been presenting their designs to the company offering the prize.

I took this as a chance to teach more about the power of thought, explaining that we can connect with others even when they're far away. I invited the children to join hands and send energy to their classmates. "Imagine we're all throwing in a big stone together and send our thoughts out into the energy field. If it's the right thing for that new classroom to come here, so be it. And if one of the other schools needs it more than us, we let go and let the Universe decide."

Teaching the children that we are part of a co-creative Universe in which we help shape the future was only a part of the project. We also explored other directions of the Medicine Wheel, sharing experiences from the East round to the West, so that children were already awakening to their relationship with all of life.

I imagine that in the tribal communities that used to follow the Medicine way, children might have gone to their elders and been told to gather stones to build a Medicine Wheel. And their teachers might have told them that the stones represented all the things of the Universe: "This one is the sun, and that one Earth. Here are the plants, and there the sacred animals." And then they might have invited the young ones to go and sit in the centre: "Feel your relationship with these powers. You're here to learn from them."

Nowadays there are many important things for children to learn, but the basics of education should be for children to come into a good relationship with their Self and with life. They will need access to their inner resources to meet the challenges they face.

Some schools are meeting this need by teaching stillness practices and mindfulness. At Park School, students learn to direct attention to the senses, and on The Children's Fire they also went to sit in their personal "magic spot" in a small woodland for a short time. It was a delight to see them learning directly from nature. Going on a mini vision quest even for ten minutes deepened their sense of relatedness with the Universe.

One of the seeds for The Children's Fire initiative came in a dreaming ceremony held in the high desert of New Mexico. This is an extraordinary landscape of dry dust, crumbling rock, and scratchy plants. It has a numinous quality, an extraordinary silence in which Spirit is as close as your breath; you feel the Unseen witnessing your every thought. The sun beats down like hammer on anvil, and the desert wind whispers its dreams.

With meticulous attention, we created a Dreamer's Lodge, using teepee poles draped with branches of aromatic piñon pine and juniper. The greenery imbued the lodge with lush life-giving energy. Added to this was our strong collective intention in the form of many red prayer ties hung among the greenery of the lodge, and we used clay Mayan figures and symbols of the mystery to create an altar around the centre fire. The overall effect was one of ineffable beauty. It was a stunning Earth Temple.

During the ceremony we fasted for three days—waking, sleeping, and tending the fire. This evoked an expanded state of consciousness in which we allowed the Universe to dream through us. We were dreaming for generations of humans yet to be born, sending the dream-seeds of how our world will be ahead of time and praying with the stars.

These are some of the dream-seeds that came:

"In the dreaming we see images of spiritual renewal, with humanity coming back into harmony with our planet.

Education has more emphasis on learning from nature. Some teaching and teacher training takes place in wilderness areas, and children have spiritual adventures, such as rites of passage."

"In schools, children remain clear about their unique identity. They learn how to focus their consciousness, how to work with energy, and how to be truly present in relationship with life. Children are brought up in self-authority, their power to author their life. They feel their kinship with all beings and how to be still and respond to life."

Experiencing these thoughts and images caused me to want to manifest them, and when I met others with similar dreams, we co-created The Children's Fire. The full effects that ripple out from that project cannot be foreseen. Consciousness is vast and mysterious. Human consciousness is multifaceted. Words may point us towards the Mystery but never illuminate it fully.

Metaphor helps, and that's where a paddling pool comes in useful. A pool of clear standing water is like the stillness of our Essence-Self, the field of unlimited potential within. When we introduce a power-thought into this field, it has an effect, especially if we are unattached to the outcome. And helping children know the Essence-Self and the power of conscious dreaming is a needed part of our evolution of consciousness.

The night after the paddling pool ceremony and our exploration of cause and effect, my phone rang. It was one of the teachers, and he'd just heard from those who'd gone to London for the new classroom competition. "They won! They won the new classroom! Those prayers we sent must have worked."

PRACTICE: To Be the Dreamer at Cause

We are constantly influencing the future with our consciousness, co-creating it with the Universe through the Law of Cause and Effect. This practice calls us to be at cause rather than at effect. This means consciously choosing what we are sending out instead of being unconsciously affected by what we're taking in.

In being a dreamer at cause we become highly conscious of this subtle realm of experience. We are co-creating our dream in every waking and sleeping moment. What we experience is neither "good" nor "bad". It is our sacred dream in the moment. When we ask ourselves how we can shape our dream into one of beauty and potential we activate the creative part of spirit. Choosing expansive high thoughts and sending compassionate loving energy into the world co-creates that dream in our reality.

Raise awareness of what you are thinking and feeling. Check in with your inner atmosphere regularly. Pause and notice what is emanating from you with every thought, word, and deed. What effects are you causing? Are they in alignment with your highest dream?

In the morning, imagine how you want your day to flow. See any obstacles clearing. Prepare your energy consciousness to meet the day's challenges and opportunities. At other times, check in with your present condition. Observe your thoughts, feelings, and body sensations to see if they are aligned with the effect you want to cause. In the evening, recall what happened with appreciation. If something disturbed you, look for the learning.

Observe without judgement, blame, or victimhood.

"Holding the high dream" means seeing the best possibility for yourself and others. By looking for the best in others you help draw it forward. When you imagine your high dream, see its benefit to life, in general; how will it help other people, plants, or animals? Release it and let the field of unlimited potential manifest in its own time and way.

Don't get caught in looking for physical evidence of your dream or the mechanics of how it will happen.

Instead, see the result in your mind's eye. Trust the unseen forces to bring it about in the best way possible.

Watch out for thoughts that contradict your dream. They may be doubts or fears such as "Oh, that's impossible." To become aware of such blocks lurking in the subconscious, imagine your dream fully manifested. Notice if there's any resistance, even subtle. If you notice fear or doubt, engage with those parts of you. Breathe and reassure them. Teach yourself what you need to learn.

Another aspect of being at cause is to be aware of what you are feeding your consciousness. Who or what are you listening to, reading, or watching?

What images, attitudes, and opinions are you consuming and how are you digesting them?

How are they affecting your wellbeing? Do they diminish or enhance life?

This practice helps us be more conscious of our influence, even on the Seventh Generation after us.

The Tower and the Birds

We experience many states of consciousness, both awake and asleep. Our journey to the centre is into more expanded states in which we know our oneness with the Divine. In these states, we know that we help shape the future with our dream-prayers. This section takes us further into this power, particularly in relation to the collective consciousness of all humans.

The renowned English writer J. B. Priestley considered his dreaming self as important as his waking self. He was inspired by dreams and by the work of J. W. Dunne, who had proposed a theory of multiple selves and parallel streams of time. This interest led Priestley to write a series of "time plays" and to experience a "big dream" that speaks to a different level of the psyche than many dreams.

In the dream Priestley is standing at the top of a very tall tower, watching multitudes of birds flying past. It is like a vast river flowing through the air; every bird in the world is part of this glorious sight.

Mysteriously, time then speeds up, and he sees generations of birds pass through their life cycles—hatching, fledging, mating, weakening, and dying. In a flash, they struggle out of their shells, try their wings, mate, and die. And he is sick at heart at the sheer futility of all this massive effort. Wouldn't it be better if none of them, if none of us, had ever been born?

The dreamer stands on his tower, utterly alone, desperately unhappy.

But then the time scale changes again, and the river of birds flows even faster. He can't make out any movement, just an immense plain sown with feathers. And through the plain there passes a flickering flame of white light, dancing, quivering, and hurrying on. With a surge of joy, he realizes that this flame is life itself, the quintessence of being, and that this flame alone is real; this alone matters.

The outer form of birds, people, or creatures yet unborn is of no import except that the inner flame of Life itself passes through them. There is no tragedy, no pity, no need for mourning, but that this white flame purifies all, and dances through us in ecstasy.

Priestley said afterwards: "I had never felt before such happiness as I knew at the end of my dream of the tower and the birds." [19]

It made a bigger impression on him than any experience he'd known, he said, and told him more about life than any book he'd ever read.

We don't often look at life from such a wide perspective as this. Our thought and attention are usually caught up with individual concerns. But from time to time, an artist working on the detail of a painting needs to stand back and look at the whole canvas. By standing back and taking a more expansive view, we can appreciate our life as a whole. Big dreams give us a glimpse beyond our personal canvas: they show us the whole art gallery.

Human consciousness is both individual and collective. Our collective consciousness means that the souls of all humans that have lived are living and will live. It is like a mighty tree—our individual lives are like leaves, each one adding energy to the trunk and branches. This tree is growing; human consciousness is evolving.

We can image the collective consciousness when we look at other species—a beehive, for example, a shoal of fish, or a termite castle. They act together with one mind, one heart. Murmurations of starlings are amazing dances, clouds of birds ebbing and flowing in the sky as one entity. The dance shapes their movement, yet each bird shapes the dance.

Another example is our own body, which is the collective consciousness of trillions of cells. Each cell is both individual and part of the collective, and each cell sends signals that have an effect on the whole. Through cooperation, they provide our vehicle for life.

The culture of Earth Medicine gives a lot of attention to the collective field of consciousness. When people sit together in a circle, everyone can see everyone else—at least with peripheral vision—and this gives a sense of the whole energy field. Like the wind, energy and consciousness are unseen, though we see the effects. Seeing the collective consciousness means looking into the unseen.

The old people of tribal communities couldn't have imagined living without being one of The People. They knew that building the collective energy field means thinking more about "us" than "me." When "we" thrive, "I" thrive because individuals flourish in collective togetherness. When the collective energy blossoms, everyone blossoms. No one is separate from the collective field.

You can observe field effects of consciousness wherever groups of people are gathered. Whether you're at the theatre, stadium, or circus, waves of feeling flow through the crowd, and part of the adventure of going to these spectacles is feeling the crowd energy, whether it's coherent or chaotic.

At more subtle levels, consciousness has field effects on an individual. A thought triggers a cascade of chemical signals throughout the body. This shifts your energy state. But thought also affects the unseen energy field that extends beyond the body and touches the energy fields of others. Every thought ripples out into the ocean of energy consciousness. Every thought affects the unseen web of interrelatedness. And every thought produces an echo, however faint it may be.

Thinking that thoughts don't matter, that we're separate from the whole, that we don't have power—these kinds of beliefs cut our power and diminish our effect.

Most of us think countless thoughts. They are beyond number, as many as the grasses growing on Earth's prairies and savannahs. They may be chaotic, incoherent, and contradictory, like background static on an untuned radio. Learning to be still and choose which thoughts to allow is a necessary part of our journey, and when we send prayer-thought with deliberation, clarity, and coherence we transmit powerful frequencies that affect the collective consciousness.

Sowing the collective dream-field with dream-seeds is done not in ordinary thought but by bringing our conscious awareness, intent, and emotional power into alignment with the Universe. We send these thoughts with gratitude and without attachment to outcome, knowing that the benevolent and generative powers of Great Mystery are ready to receive them:

I see the collective consciousness awakening to the beauty of the Earth. I imagine sacred humans realizing their oneness and their power to change the collective dream. I see the children growing with hope and happiness in their hearts. Let it be so.

PRACTICE: Sowing the Dream Field with Beauty

This dreaming contemplation is intended to expand the collective consciousness and bring us back into alignment with the planet.

Start with intentional breathing to connect with the light of the Universe. Breathe in slowly, imagining light pouring into you. Let this energy shimmer through every cell in your body. See it emanating from you as you breathe out.

Now expand your consciousness, and feel your connection with the Universe. Feel the source within you, and let it heal and resource your inner world.

Generate appreciation and gratitude for the beauty that life has given you. Call to mind something you appreciate, and let that feeling expand.

Once this energy feels strong, you may also like to contemplate things that you find challenging. Look for the benefit or the aspect in them that you can appreciate.

All things are connected in the web of life. See your Self connected with the many other dreamers who are holding the dream of oneness. Imagine that you are weaving the web of expanded consciousness in our human world.

See this web spreading through the collective consciousness.

Knowing that every thought is a prayer, what dreams do you send for our world? They may be of places for wildlife to thrive;

clean air and water; harmony and peace; the chance for people to heal and learn. How do you want to affect the people around you? The people you live with, neighbours, community, strangers in the street, even people in the wider world? What do you want to dream into being?

Close this dreaming space by counting down from 10 to 1. Take a breath, and come back into waking consciousness.

Whispers of the Oracle

In this last section of the Northwest, we'll consider another facet of the dreaming consciousness: how we can "read" the Medicine signs of the dreamfield. I'm at Cumae, a ruined Greek city on the coast of Italy. People used to come here from all over the ancient world to consult its oracle. Through the trees in front of me is the silver sea, shimmering in the sunlight. To my left is an entrance into the rock, a long tunnel leading to the cave of the Sybil, the Oracle of Cumae. I start along the tunnel.

Nobody knows now why the ancients cut the tunnel in this funny shape; it's a trapezoid that narrows towards the ceiling. But it is known that signs hewn into its walls are symbols of a lunar cult, and the prophetess at the far end served Apollo.

Pilgrims came to the oracle to ask questions. How would they have felt as they approached her? She was known as the Sybil and would go into frenzied ecstasy during which, it was said, the god rode her like a mare. This divine madness enabled her to see through the veil of time, and she sang out people's fate in verses. Those who came for a consultation would probably have quaked as they crept along the tunnel.

The story goes that the Sybil had made a deal with Apollo. In return for her virginity, he granted her one wish. She picked up a handful of sand and asked to live as many years as she held grains of sand. So she lived a great length of time; there was only ever one Sybil. In this way, Cumae was different from oracles like Delphi or Dodona, which were run by a succession of priestesses and priests.

All around the ancient Mediterranean, there were sacred centres where you could consult a seer. Since then, oracles have had a long decline in Western culture, at least until recently when oracle cards and readings have become popular. But the "oracular" state of consciousness is latent in most of us. We have the potential to intuit, to read the signs, to see beyond the surface into deeper levels of reality. Our ability to translate messages from life is inherent, and we can develop it. But how?

It may be that pilgrims to Cumae came with such expectation and yearning for insight that whatever the Sybil sang, it triggered their deeper knowing. They believed the Divine spoke through her directly about their concerns, and reality responds to our beliefs. If we don't believe that life responds to us, it won't, or at least we won't notice when it does. If we believe that life is full of consciousness, and we're in relationship with it, it's easier to pay attention when it gives us a sign.

Where do signs come from? Whatever name you call their source—Apollo, Universe, the Superconscious—they are of the Mystery. They come to us not from logical thought processes but from levels of consciousness beyond our conscious control. Daydreaming and dozing allow us to dip into these realms, and night dreams immerse us in them deeply. Repetitive actions such as walking, canoeing, or dance may also allow us to access these dreamy realms.

One evening years ago, for example, I was with friends drumming by a fire in a teepee in Wales. I began to dance and let the djembe move my body and carry my consciousness deeper. I found myself wrestling with a huge green anaconda, while fully aware of my physical location. When the drumming finished, I sat down feeling whole, complete and blessed by this dream-sign. I had been campaigning for the rainforest, feeling stressed about deforestation, and I felt the anaconda spirit had come with healing energy.

Signs come in many ways, not only in the many forms of divination such as cards, bones, clouds, tea leaves, and animals but in voices overheard in crowds, body symptoms, and computer quirks. To make meaning out of them it helps to relate them to our concerns and questions.

Questions can be containers in which to receive messages and signs. The Medicine path has been called the way of the question. At school, we're taught it's good to have answers, but answers may close the door on inquiry, while questions open it. They expand our perspective and lead us into deeper communion with the Mystery. As Einstein said: "The important thing is not to stop questioning . . . to comprehend a little of this mystery every day."

When we hold a question, we activate our spirit to quest into the Mystery, and this supports our journey into wholeness.

Some years ago, my wife and I were wondering whether to buy a flat. For some time, we discussed the arguments for and against, then decided to consult an oracle. At the time, we had my father's library of history books lining one wall of our living room. Holding the question strongly in mind, we closed our eyes and each reached for a book, opening at random and pointing to a line. My line was about a rebellion in France in which property owners were pelted with mud, and hers was even clearer: "The tower was built on sand." We didn't buy the flat.

A way to work with the technology of the question is first to formulate it clearly, perhaps with "How?" or "What is needed?" Questions beginning with "Why?" can lead us into a lot of reasoning with the brain-mind. The oracular consciousness is beyond reason. I used to find it difficult to trust intuition because I tended to rely on reason and be busy in thought. It became easier after I worked with meditation and other presence practices because presence and stillness create space in us in which to receive.

The oracular consciousness is a receptive state in which we allow ourselves to be penetrated by the Mystery.

As we hold a question, we hold the basket of the Self open. We can be relaxed but alert to whatever attracts our attention through sight, sound, smell, feelings, or body sensations. Signs may come from places we least expect them. Holding the question means yielding to the dream of the Universe to teach us what we need to see at this time.

To translate oracles and signs, we need to allow them to touch our sensitivity. Let us set aside the one in us who deals only in nuts and bolts and demands strict definition. Instead let's open the magic of myth and metaphor and listen to the poet within all of us. Let us be at ease with not knowing and trust the unknown to inform us.

What is the kernel within the dream-seed, the spirit-essence behind that which has moved us? Feeling into this essence and allowing it to penetrate us, we begin to look through its eyes, hear with its ears, and speak with its mouth. We can then look back at our personal Self, deliver the message from our Infinite Self, and translate its inspiration into resolution.

In this way, we don't need to let the divine trance ride us in the way Apollo rode the Sybil. The poet Virgil said that she used to pull her hair out as she sang people's fate. She also suffered in another way—a way that shows the truth of the adage: "Be careful what you wish for." She asked Apollo for the gift of great longevity but didn't specify eternal youth. So as each year passed with the falling of leaves, she grew older and older and withered smaller and smaller. After centuries she was so small that she lived in a jar; eventually only her voice remained.

In Cumae, I felt the power of place before I entered the tunnel. When I reached her cave at the end, I sensed its mystery, though it had long stood empty. If there was any whisper of her still remaining, I took its meaning to be to write about oracles and tell her story.

PRACTICE: Holding a Question

Holding a question means keeping a question open in your consciousness for a period of time.

Often we close off questions with the first answer. Holding a question changes our relationship with the dreaming Universe. We begin to see all of life as an oracle and open to a new level of understanding.

Holding a question does not mean trying to work it out with rational thinking. A question is a container, like a bowl, basket, or even the dish of a radio telescope. It allows us to receive messages in response.

Formulate your question simply. "How?" or "What is needed?" are good openings for this. Make it an open question that does not expect a "right" answer or a simple yes or no. It may even lead you to more questions.

You may like to write your question down or speak it aloud to the Universe. Then hold it for a period of time—anything from a few minutes to several months. Let life be your oracle and gather the messages that come in response.

Responses come in many different ways, both while you're awake and in night dreams. Notice what attracts your attention and intuit its meaning in relation to your question. Introspect, for example, by imagining that you are the essence of that which attracted your attention. If you were it, what would you say to your everyday Self about this question?

Weaving the Web of Expanded Consciousness

North: Heart

Awakening the six realms of consciousness of the previous chapters has a cumulative effect and enables us to open our heart-mind. This is an essential step on our journey because the heart-mind gives us the wisdom and energy consciousness to move through the global crisis.

In the North of the Medicine Wheel is air—wind. Air is a mystery that's in and all around us, invisible yet visible in the blueness of sky. It is the azure veil that surrounds our planet, Mother Earth's aura, which gives life to all her offspring. It's the air that provides oxygen, the force we take into our lungs, blood, and cells.

The heart is far more than a mechanism. It is a power centre, an ancient organ of consciousness that has evolved over numberless generations and is common to all animals. For animals, it is the organ of instinct. They don't spend a lot of time thinking; they know. This knowing is the essence of heart intelligence.

Consciousness is more complex in humans than in other animals. Of all the offspring of life, it has been said, humans alone have the power to choose to override instinct. Choice is our gift and challenge. The challenge is to come to know our relationship with the rest of life, and the gift is to access the clear courage that our heart-knowing brings us.

Heart-knowing is the human equivalent of instinct. It's different to brain-thinking. Heart-knowing mobilizes our inner resources—will, creativity, emotional power, and so on. It calls us to step forward with courage. Of all our organs of consciousness, it's the heart that activates healing—for our Self and others. Because it is also, of course, the primary organ for love to flow through.

We start this exploration of the North with **The Way of the Animal Teachers,** because the sacred animals reflect much that we need to remember about the heart. They teach us about our relationship with life and with the centre of the Self.

It can be difficult to know the clarity of our heart when our emotions are stuck. We need to use emotional power—to become present and hear the message of our feelings and the lessons of the situation. Then we can bring emotional energy up to our heart. Balancing the South–North axis in this way enables our access to higher wisdom and empowers us to act in life-enhancing ways.

The second section, **The Heart of Courage,** explores courage and clarity. These are faculties of the heart-mind that are vital for our journey to the centre and for our effectiveness in daily life.

Activating the heart-mind creates an energy force field that can evoke high consciousness in ourselves and others. This is true charisma, and Mahatma Gandhi is an example of this. He generated the force field of the heart-mind to effect change in consciousness and in the world. **Soul Force** explores this theme and tells his story.

We block our heart-knowing when our consciousness is full of brain-thinking. We can enslave ourselves with ideas and eclipse the light of the heart with ideology. But we can also free our heart by using the tools of awareness, intention, dreaming, and heart strategy. **How Much Is Enough?** tells Rachel's story of breaking free of limiting beliefs.

The Way of the
Animal Teachers

There are moments when nature looks you straight in the eye. In its timeless presence, you can't hide, you can't pretend, you can only be in the raw not-knowing of who you are.

I am scrambling on the dry rock of a mountain outcrop. Far into the distance spreads the sunlit plain; a few miles away is the place of Buddha's enlightenment, Bodh Gaya.

This morning I have been lower down the mountain, at the Mahakala caves, where he spent years fasting and meditating. And before that, I have been travelling in India for months, never far from multitudinous crowds and dense population. But there's no one else here in this desert place.

Then I sense a presence. I am not alone. Just yards away on a crag, a huge owl pierces me with its gaze. I stay, for an eternal moment, transfixed, skewered by its stare. Its orange eyes flay me to the core, strip layers of thought, peel away all ideas of who I thought I was. The owl and I are one: eternal Mystery.

Then my humanness starts up again. Perhaps I can get a bit closer. I look down at the ground to move, look up, and the owl is gone, the silent sky empty.

Thinking back to this incident across the years, I see that I wasn't conscious of the fullness of the owl's gift. Yes, I was moved. I felt reverence, and I thought I was lucky to see it. But I didn't think I'd received a "sign." Now I know that when an animal spirit comes to you, pay attention, especially if it's doing something unusual, as this was. Eagle-owl usually hunts by night; when it comes in broad daylight, it brings a dream message. I didn't trust my intuition to interpret it at the time, but now I believe the owl was calling me to dream deeper.

Before going to the Mahakala caves, I had been on a retreat in Bodh Gaya, spending long hours in meditation. That spiritual quest had opened a space for my yearning to come forth and for my heart to reach out to the animal spirits. The dreaming mind of eagle-owl had responded by fetching me into its presence. I wasn't conscious of it, but I was being called to journey into the subterranean realms of the psyche. When fate knocks on your door, you only need to open it a crack.

At the surface level of mind, things are just what they are. But there are ancient depths where myth and metaphor speak of the primal. When we look in the great mirror of creation and see the reflections of animal spirits, they are symbols of this. They come in the uncluttered clarity of the heart to remind us of power—the power that flows through their veins and ours. At the prosaic level, they're just animals; at the poetic, though, they offer us shards of raw power. They've never forgotten their connection with the web of life, and they reawaken this in us, insofar as we open to its caress.

It's been said that alone of Mother Earth's offspring, we humans do not innately know our oneness with the web of life or understand the balance of give and take. But we are endowed with greater choice than other animals. We can choose, for example, how to interpret what happens. We can choose where to direct our attention. Animals act on instinct; we can choose to override it.

The gift of choice challenges us to overcome the illusion of separation from life. We meet this challenge by coming into heart-wisdom to make choices that bring balance. Animals can help us learn to do this, because they come from the heart and our consciousness is close enough to theirs for their heart to awaken ours.

We have distanced ourselves from them by feeling superior. Superiority separates. We have beliefs and ideologies that justify superiority, but these keep us from the essence-truth of our heart. Our consciousness is more complex, and we are special, but that doesn't make us inherently better—all species are special.

Animals show a purity of being, a purity of nature. They are true to their essence. They are who they are. An eagle has no confusion, only a powerful knowing. It is a feathered lord of the sky whose heart is clear. It doesn't wonder whether it can be bothered to fly; it flies. This clarity of heart is never lost to humans, but we can obscure it, occult it, lose access to it. We can forget our Essence-Self. The animal powers remind us of the simpler truth of our hearts. At the deepest level they teach us to be true to our own Self.

Power comes in many forms. I'm not speaking of social, political, or military power—power "over" things; I mean personal power—the power from within. The eight directions of the Medicine Wheel, our eight intelligences, are portals through which power flows. And each animal has its own Medicine and teaches a different nuance of power.

The sacred animals are reflections of the purity of who we are, and their teachings show the way to our wholeness. We honour them with gratitude and by making space for relationship with this animal power. We can come to know the animal through study—how it feeds, breeds, and shelters—but also through feeling it in our heart, body, and energy field. We need to trust the clarity of our own heart-knowing, because our relationship with this animal power is unique.

So the Medicine of an eagle-owl is different from that of other kinds of owl. To me, eagle-owl is a teacher that connects night dreams and day dreams. The piercing vision of its orange eyes represents the power to see beyond the surface to the essence of things. Our primal mind sees animals in everything—glowing in the embers of fire, riding in clouds upon the wind, or etched in the faces of stones.

One night in New Mexico, I dreamed of a green rattlesnake, a Mojave viper. I'd seen it the day before, sliding, silent, and deadly, flowing like a green spear across the earth. A friend skilled in snake handling had carried it away from our camp. In the dream, I carried a rattlesnake into a museum gift shop. The assistant shouted: "Get that thing out of here." At that point, the serpent turned its head and stung me on my left hand, but I knew in the dream that being thus envenomed was healing, not slaying.

Snake has been my "shadow animal," the beast that most calls forth my fear, and I felt the transformative power of this dream. The shop assistant was the socialized part of me, working in the safe intellectual space of a museum. But the serpent represented my undomesticated wildness and was bringing me into balance by biting my nondominant side.

We humans have great Medicine; our powers of reason, reflection, and analysis are tremendous. But to journey to our centre, we need to balance these with our primal power and remember the deep knowing of the heart. The brain-mind can get us lost in the maze, lost in confusion, lost in forgetting who we really are. The heart never gets lost or confused. And the clarity of the heart is our next subject.

PRACTICE: The Medicine of Your Animal Teacher

Animals are sacred expressions of the life force. Like us, they carry the Divine within them. The spirits of animals come to us in many ways, in diverse levels of dreaming by day and night. When an animal comes to you, particularly in an unusual way, accept that it is bringing you a teaching.

How do you discern its message?

Yield and let it come in. Introspect and intuit its message. Animals are never other than their Essence-Self. So they teach us of authenticity and of being true to ourselves.

Study the animal. Learn about its strengths, patterns, and characteristics. But study not only with intellect but with dreaming. Use imagination to deepen your relationship with it. Contemplate: What does the animal reflect about your Self? Medicine power comes through relationship, and as you learn about the animal's medicine you learn about your own.

Appreciation opens the heart, so express appreciation to the animal-spirit.

Your relationship with it is two-way. How can you give back to it? Create things that represent your relationship with the animal spirit. Do this with your own hands. Imbue these creations with attention and intention.

You might choose pictures, sculptures, fetishes—anything can represent it. Give this object your attention. Treat it with reverence.

Call on the animal regularly. For example, call it to mind before you fall asleep. You can ask it to lead you into your night dreams and reveal something about your Self. Or you can call it before an important meeting such as an interview.

The Heart of Courage

The heart knows our soul connection with life. Awakening the heart enables us to remember this. The world shimmers with luminosity, but it's through the heart that we appreciate this, not ordinary thought. When we sense this shimmering, we glimpse a realm of consciousness vaster than the one we usually inhabit.

Opening the door of the heart to this realm connects us with all abundance, all potential, all wisdom. These resources are within us. But how do we open this door?

A friend of mine, Toni, had a special white silk scarf that had been blessed by the Dalai Lama. One day she came home to find it missing. It turned out that Max, her flatmate's boyfriend, had "borrowed" it and left it somewhere around the city.

"Don't worry," he shrugged. "I'll just get you another one."

She was stunned by his flippancy. She couldn't find the words to respond. For a day or two she stewed in her own juice. Her anguish tangled her up in an emotional complex, because she thought that the Dalai Lama would not want her to be angry or feel attached to a scarf. Instead of anger she got depressed, telling herself that people had no respect for her boundaries.

Then she rang me. I'd been a guide for her before and knew that she lacked self-confidence. I knew my own pattern of shrinking from confrontation but also knew that the heart gives us courage. Our heart knows how to do what needs to be done and speak what needs to be spoken. When we follow our heart-knowing we clear the energy in and around us.

At first she sounded numb, but as she told me the story, her tears started to flow. I asked her what would happen if she challenged him, and it brought out her resistance to challenging anyone, a deep-rooted fear that came from early childhood. She'd never spoken about it before, and I told her that I felt honoured that she trusted me enough to do so in this moment.

I was aware that we were working in the South of the Wheel—with emotions and trust—and that she needed to access the power in the opposite direction: the courage and clarity of the North. But to do so, she would also need the Southeast energy of present awareness to see deeply into her current condition.

We took some deep breaths together, and I guided her into a mini meditation on the breath. As she began to feel calmer, I suggested she focus on the breath going into her heart.

After a few minutes I asked her: "What does the clarity of your heart say to do about this situation?"

There was resolution in her voice as she responded: "If I don't say something, this is going to happen again. It's not just about the scarf; this is about me. I just don't want people walking over me. I'm going to speak to him about this, come what may. I want to be free.'

She was clearly resolved at this moment, but I knew from experience how easily the fearful in us can come back later. A line from Shakespeare flashed into my mind:

> *Our doubts are traitors,*
> *And make us lose the good we oft might win*
> *By fearing to attempt.*[20]

So I spoke about this, and she said she'd practise coming back to her breath and heart. "If I do that, there's no way I'm gonna let the fear take over again." She was determined.

The next night, as we'd agreed, she called me again. This time her tears were of triumph, not despair. She said she'd been practising the heart-breath off and on all day. Even so, a part of her had wanted to run away when Max had come home.

"My heart was beating like crazy, but I told myself, *No, I'm going to do this.*"

She'd asked Max if they could speak, and they'd sat together. She'd told him how she'd been feeling, but she hadn't thrown her anger at him.

"Once I'd started, I felt clear and centred, and I didn't just lose it with him. I spoke through my heart about my feelings, and it touched him. I told him why the scarf mattered, but I also asked him to respect my wishes, and he agreed."

By accessing her heart-mind, Toni was able to quieten herself enough to see beyond her fear. She accessed the courage to take her next step. It was a personal victory that empowered her with greater self-respect. Facing our inner tigers with courage turns their wrath to benevolence.

Just as everyone has fear, everyone has courage. Courage is heart energy that enables us to take the action needed. (The word comes from the French for heart, *coeur*.) Our heart knows directly, without needing to work things out. This clarity makes it easy to move into action.

Fear is a primal energy that alerts and readies us for action. In animals, it leads to actions of fight, flight, or freeze. As humans, it can cause us to freeze; we can become stuck in thinking and confused. But when we bring it up to our heart, we can feel courage and clarity.

Our heart-knowing informs us of what is needed. It enables us to speak our truth clearly and to express emotion in life-affirming ways. When anger comes through the heart, it is clean and clear; it doesn't diminish. It pierces, not like a wounding arrow but like an acupuncture needle enabling energy to flow. It pierces the limitations we put on ourselves. That's why Max was able to hear Toni's words.

When our heart is closed, we don't need to judge ourselves. Judging only tightens its closure. We cannot control the heart or force it open. But we can use the pattern Toni followed—deepening into stillness and awareness first. Accepting our present condition allows it to change.

When we face a big choice, we may think we have to reason it out with our brain-mind. Our brain gives us pro and con, for and against, advantage and disadvantage. But the heart-mind *knows.* By listening to the decisive clarity of the heart, our decisions become simple.

It takes courage to speak out when something is out of balance. When we challenge the status quo, we challenge ourselves. We challenge our sense of who we thought we were.

What are the wings on which the heart soars? It is tethered by habits of domesticated thinking; stress, overwhelm, and slavery are its fetters. We unleash it by suspending these patterns. It soars on sensitivity to the touch of the shimmering. Directing passion to the heart—joy, lust, grief, desire, anger—breaks through to the raw vitality of our Essence. In rawness, we sense the shimmering that courses through our veins and Universe. We glide on its rising thermals.

The heart-mind evokes and calls us forward. When it is aligned with universal truth, it generates a force field, and that's what we're going to explore next.

PRACTICE: Opening the Heart of Courage

We may have been living mainly from our brain-mind, but we can train ourselves to balance this with heart-mind. This is especially helpful when we're facing a choice or challenge and need courage and clarity.

A way to access heart-knowing is to follow the sequence of the Medicine Wheel and touch each of the earlier six energies in turn, starting in the East.

Take a deep breath with each one—as you awaken the unlimited potential of your spirit, as you come into stillness and high awareness, as you feel your emotional power, as you remember the truth of who you are, as you honour the healing power of your body, and as you recognize your power to co-create the future with the Universe.

Activate each of these powers with the breath, and know that these vast resources are within you.

Now, take a deep breath into your heart and feel its direct knowing. Take another deep breath and know your connection with the sky.

Continue to breathe deeply. As you widen the aperture of the heart with each breath, you are opening to universal wisdom.

Let universal wisdom inform your choice of how to move. What does this clarity of heart say is needed to bring wholeness to your current situation? What action or words are needed for the good of all?

A path is made by walking and practising this sequence regularly. It makes the path to your heart-knowing easily accessible.

Soul Force

 Mahatma Gandhi showed the power of the heart-mind in action. What can his life teach us about this power and about peace consciousness? I went to Madurai to learn about him. It was in this ancient city in South India that Gandhi gave up Western clothes and adopted peasant dress. The city has a Gandhi Memorial Centre, and I spent several days there reading about him in the library and looking around the museum. Among the exhibits was the blood-stained *dhoti* he was wearing when he was shot.

A couple of months later, I was back in Delhi. I went to the house he was staying in when he died and saw the spot where his last footsteps are marked in red. I learned that he'd gone there during the partition of India and Pakistan and had been fasting. It was a time of much bloodshed, and his intention had been to inspire peace in the warring factions. In Madurai, I'd been touched by the beauty of his words. Now, I was struck by the violence with which his walk of peace had ended.

There'd been assassination attempts on him before, and he said: "If someone were to end my life by putting a bullet through me . . . and I met his bullet without a groan and breathed my last, taking God's name—then alone would I make good my claim to be the man of God."

The next afternoon, he went into the gardens to pray with the homeless refugees camping there. Still weak from the fast, he was supported by two of his women relatives on either side. As he approached the crowd, he came face to face with his killer, and they exchanged the Hindu gesture of greeting, the *namaste*. Then the younger man drew his pistol, shot him three times, and Gandhi uttered his last words: "*Hey Ram* (Oh, God)."

Ghandi's death ushered in a period of relative peace between the communities. It was a measure of people's love for him that they felt united in grief. As his follower Jawaharlal Nehru said: "The light has gone out of our lives."

When you make the gesture of *namaste,* you bring your palms together in front of your heart and face. It means "I salute the Divinity in you." Behind this gesture is the belief that everyone carries the spark of the Divine within them, in their heart-centre. When I honour the sacred in you, I honour it in me, and I call it forward in consciousness. This attitude was fundamental to Gandhi and to his effect on the world.

He dedicated his life to calling forward the Divine in himself and others. It's well known that he was a leader of India's movement to independence, but his idea of independence wasn't simply "home rule;" it was "self rule."

India's national motto is "Truth alone triumphs, not falsehood." It comes from an ancient Hindu text, the Mundaka Upanishad, which continues: "When you realize you are the Self, supreme source of light, supreme source of love, you transcend the duality of life and enter the unitive state."[21]

It was this "unitive state" that Gandhi aspired to. As he put it himself: "There is an indefinable mysterious power that pervades everything." He spent his life exploring that power and conducting "experiments with truth."[22]

As a young man, Gandhi trained in English law in London and practised in South Africa. But he read Leo Tolstoy's book, The *Kingdom of Heaven Is within You*, and it changed his life. Tolstoy had been inspired by Jesus but thought many people had missed Jesus's point. He wrote that "Love is the only way to rescue humanity from all ills," and argued for non-violent protests to bring social change and overcome poverty and war.[23]

Gandhi's method of campaigning was called *satyagraha*, which means "soul-force" or "truth-force." It is a force in consciousness, and Gandhi expressed it through non-violent civil disobedience. This force emanates from the heart-mind when the other energy centres—emotions, will, brain-mind, and so on—are aligned with the heart, creating an intentional field of energy consciousness aligned with the Universe.

To be aligned with the Universe we need to transcend the illusion of separate, competing egos and connect with the Infinite Self. By doing so, we do not feed feelings of opposition or hostility; the heart does not have enemies. In the field of wholeness, there is diversity but no enemy. The root meaning of the word enemy is "un-friend" or "not-love," and the field of the heart is essentially one of love, in the biggest sense of that word.

Non-violent civil disobedience is usually in resistance to something—racism or deforestation, for example. Paradoxically, its practitioners are in non-resistance. They're aligned with the Universe. Because they don't fight back, there's nothing to fight against. If you do fight them, you find you are fighting the Universe. How can you "win"? And by emanating love through the heart, they concentrate inner power rather than "power-over." This makes them very awkward to move out of the way.

Love has different faces. The ancient Greeks distinguished different kinds of love: *eros* for sexual love, *storge* for love between friends, and *agape* for universal love. Gandhi's love was agape; he loved the Divine and honoured the sacredness of all humanity. It was this that made *satyagraha* so powerful.

He was well aware of the influence of love on his friends. He didn't just want to beat the British; he wanted the British to grow in consciousness. Love can be tough, and Gandhi challenged them to grow with tough love. By emanating a powerful field of love and truth through the heart, he evoked these energies in others. This is an example of the evocative power of the heart-mind.

In 1942, Gandhi launched the Quit India campaign and said this:

I can say that I have never felt any hatred. As a matter of fact, I feel myself to be a greater friend of the British now than ever before. One reason is that they are today in distress. My very friendship, therefore, demands that I should try to save them from their mistakes. . . .

At a time when I may have to launch the biggest struggle of my life,
I may not harbour hatred against anybody.

Soul-force isn't only for great causes like ending imperialism or slavery. We can apply the field of the heart-mind to individual needs and wants, providing we align them with the common good. We can get the heart-mind behind our intentions—our spiritual practice, for example, or our healing or creative projects. When we bring our visions to the heart with the sense that "this needs to happen," it supports us to follow through in spite of challenges and disappointments that come to us along the way. When any of us align our heart with universal truth or love, we create a resonance in the field and draw everyone's vibration towards it, adding to the transformation of human consciousness.

Apart from Ghandi's blood-stained dhoti, another exhibit in the Gandhi Museum in Madurai is a letter from Gandhi to Hitler, written in pencil and dated 23 July, 1939. The letter began, "Dear Friend" and asked Hitler not to go to war but to pursue his aims through non-violence. He signed it "Your sincere friend, M. K. Gandhi." We'll never know what effect it might have had on Hitler's heart, because it was never delivered by the British authorities.

Years later, I found out that Martin Luther King had been an earlier visitor to the Gandhi Memorial Centre. He'd gone there as a pilgrim, following in the footsteps of the Mahatma. His own use of non-violence and soul-force was partly inspired by Gandhi.

It can be tempting to project our brilliance onto charismatic individuals like Gandhi and King, but we shouldn't deny our own potential. When we admire qualities in another, it's because the same qualities are in us—at least, potentially. The unitive state and heart-mind power aren't out of our reach, but we may need to free ourselves of the limiting beliefs that stand in our way. And that is the subject of the next section.

PRACTICE: The Breath of Love

The essence of breath comes from the sky, which is part of the energy field surrounding our planet. Clouds come and go, but behind them, the sky is always clear.

Imagine your heart as clear as the sky. As the wind clears the sky, let breath clear your consciousness. Be open to the knowing of your heart and to any wisdom it may reveal to you.

Breathe slowly and deeply, with attention on the heart. Placing your hand there helps your focus to rest there. Draw in the clarity of sky, and feel oxygen filling your heart with vitality.

Let your heart be like the sun at midday, rays of high vibration radiating through your system, loving, healing, energizing. You can visualize your connection with the sun as you do this—breathing in sunlight to the heart, breathing it out to your energy-centres, and to other life-forms around you.

A variation of this is breathing in love from the trees, landscape, sky and breathing love back to them.

You can also emanate love to strangers in the street. Appreciate the uniqueness of each person. Find something to love about them; whatever state their consciousness is in, their core is love. All of us have, or will have, challenges, loss, and disappointment, joy and ecstasy, triumph and disaster. All of us are on a journey of learning; we're all drops in the great river of humanity.

As our heart-mind vibrates with love, we generate resonance in the hearts of others, drawing them into that vibration. This adds to the transformation of the collective consciousness.

How Much Is Enough

We are patterned beings. We have patterns of emotion, thought, and behaviour. As children, we take in patterns of belief from the people around us, and this enables us to grow into the world. But by the time we're adult, these belief structures may be limiting our growth. They may be keeping us from the clarity of our hearts.

As adults, we can choose to review our beliefs; we can change them in order to keep growing into the fullness of our potential.

Here is the story of one woman's transformation and her steps towards freedom of the heart.

There was never enough—not enough money, not enough time, not enough space, not enough . . . love. The only thing Rachel had enough of was overwhelm.

She'd been walking by the river, tears flowing like the rain around her. It was then that she saw the fox. Standing on the edge of the trees, looking at her, the fox seemed very close. She felt its dark eyes seeing into her soul.

A couple of nights later, she woke up from a vivid dream. At first, she was following the fox through a wasteland of factories and smoke but then they crossed a bridge and went into a building that seemed to have many rooms. It turned out to be her home, but there were builders in it. They'd ripped out all the walls and furnishings. They were renovating it.

The next day she met an old friend, Robbie, and told her the dream. Robbie invited her to go with her to a talk the following Friday, and they went together. It was unlike any talk she'd been to before. The main speaker was part Finnish, part American, a tall woman with green eyes. Her presence compelled attention, and she introduced herself as Golden Rose. She explained that this was a Medicine name she'd received when she was an apprentice.

She began speaking about Indigenous wisdom and how people could use it to create wellbeing. Then she invited each of the people to tell the story of why they'd come.

It made Rachel awkward to speak in public, but everyone listened intently as she told of her meeting with the fox and of her dream. Then Golden Rose guided them into various activities, and by the end of the evening it seemed to Rachel that the people in the room were no longer strangers. She felt something unusual—a sense of belonging.

Golden Rose was introducing a two-year training journey and invited those who'd come to consider joining it. In the days and nights that followed, Rachel wrestled with the idea of joining Robbie on this adventure. She decided to try the first weekend.

While on the training, she learned many tools of self-knowledge. She found herself doing things she'd never imagined—making masks, drumming, sculpting with clay, performing ritual theatre, and doing hands-on healing. There was a lot of laughter and an amazing feeling of support in the group.

Rachel was in awe of Golden Rose. She was charismatic, wise, and powerful but also loving, with an infectious sense of humour. At the end of one of the weekends Rachel summoned up the courage to tell her so, and Golden Rose responded:

> **Thank you. But the only reason you see these things in me is because they are in you. You have these qualities in potential, and you're growing into them. Just keep showing up for this training and do your work.**

The "work" meant practising tools of consciousness. And it meant looking deeply into her patterns of thought, word, and action to see which patterns would lead to her flowering and which ones would take her somewhere else. Golden Rose had told her students:

How you experience life is shaped by your consciousness, and your consciousness is shaped by your beliefs. If you want to be free and stand in your greatness, pull your beliefs up from your subconscious and have a damn good look at them. Only that will give you the power to change and become more of who you really are.

Rachel was sure she wanted to "stand in greatness," but she just couldn't see the beliefs that were holding her back. They seemed so "true" for her that she couldn't see that they were beliefs. But she was diligent about observing herself and using tools to expand her perspective. Gradually, she surfaced a core belief that she simply wasn't enough.

As a child at home, she'd taken in the message that she wasn't old enough; at school, the idea that she wasn't clever enough. She noticed that adverts gave her the feeling that she wasn't beautiful enough or didn't have enough. She'd worked hard to make up for her inadequacy, but nothing was ever enough for her inner judge. She told this to her teacher, and Golden Rose said:

This feeling of lack is one of the biggest dis-eases in our world. Because of this we're unable to share with those who genuinely need more. Because of this we degrade our life-support system, the Earth's resources. Because of this so many of Mother Earth's children are living in mental and physical slavery.

"Yes," said Rachel, "but I still want things. I'd like a Medicine name, for example."

Golden Rose replied:

It's not wrong to want things; it's part of being human. But when we always want more and don't appreciate what we have . . . Instead, when we remember our relationship with Self and life it gives us a sense of enoughness. Then we can live in beauty. You're beginning now to heal the sense of lack, and when more of us do this, we'll begin to solve many of our problems and create peace on Earth. Oh, and you can have a Medicine name. You need to call on life to show it you.

Her assistant, White Phoenix, was sitting next to her. He said: "I often think, How much is enough? You know the answer?" He laughed. "Just one more!"

After that Rachel began to give herself an easier time. She cultivated a sense of abundance to replace her old belief structure, often taking time in nature to feel the life force in the elements and in herself. Meditation helped her notice the thoughts that led to feeling inadequate. She created an affirmation:

"I am whole and complete, and I am learning."

Gradually, she created new neural pathways for her thoughts to flow along in life-affirming ways.

At the end of the training journey, she was invited to go on vision quest in the north of Scotland. She spent three days at a spot in the mountains overlooking a loch. The last night was cold, but she kept a fire going and luxuriated in the abundance of stars overhead.

At one point, she looked up and saw a weird luminosity in the sky. It made her stomach clench. Was she losing it? Glowing green curtains of light were changing to maroon in the silent immensity, and the hairs on her neck prickled. Now there was blood-red around the edges. It was the northern lights, the fabled aurora. Enraptured, she didn't even notice the tears of joy flowing down her cheeks.

Back in camp, she told her story. She said the aurora had felt like an affirmation from the Universe.

Golden Rose reflected back to her:

"I think you're right. You know in Finland we have a name for the lights. It comes from an old story. We call it the fox fire."

"Yes," said Rachel. "That's my spirit name, and I'm ready to claim it. I am Fox Fire."

PRACTICE: Stalk Your Limiting Beliefs

The aim of this practice is to bring to the surface any core beliefs about yourself and life that may have held you back. Awareness gives you the choice of whether to change them. Three helpers that raise awareness are intention, observation, and expanded consciousness.

Early each day, set your intention to observe your core patterns and beliefs. ("Observe" does not mean "judge;" judgement tends to keep things hidden.) Many of our thoughts are expressions of belief structures, so use stillness practices to become more aware of your thoughts. Particularly notice the thought-phrases you say to yourself when you are emotionally impacted. Or if you realize that you're feeling low, trace your thinking back to find the thoughts that led to this mood.

Record your observations in a journal. A way to do this is by reviewing your day in the evening before sleep. Observe anything unresolved or complex. Look deeply to see the belief structures behind what happened, and note down your observations. Periodically review your journal, and notice any patterns. Notice any repeating circumstances that trigger a limiting pattern.

What could you do differently?

Many other spiritual practices support stalking your beliefs. Some of those already described in this book include the stillness practices "Sculpting Your Landscape of Thought," "To Be the Dreamer at Cause in Our World," and "Golden Woman / Golden Man." Use them to take yourself into expanded consciousness. Any contracting thought or belief will then be even more apparent because of the contrast.

When you have brought any limiting beliefs to the surface, stay present and open-hearted towards your Self. Breathe into your heart. Do you choose to change this belief? If so, create a plan of healing. Include what you need to teach yourself and what will support you.

Emanating Heart Wisdom from Source

ENERGY

8

Northeast: Energy

The Northeast is the direction of energy, movement, and change. It is where we check whether all our energies are aligned. If they are, we feel enthusiasm, integrity, and vitality. In our spiral journey to the centre of the Self, we have awakened each realm of consciousness in turn: in the East, realizing that we are spirit, part of all spirit; in the Southeast, heightening awareness of life through presence; in the South, trusting our emotional power and opening to diversity; in the Southwest, guided by our true identity; in the West, honouring the body; in the Northwest, dreaming the future in relation to the Universe; in the North, accessing the courage and clarity of our heart-mind. We need each of these to transform our individual and collective consciousness.

The moon is a powerful symbol of movement and change. Always waxing or waning, the moon is the cause of so much movement on our planet; the ocean tides, for example, and the rise of water in plants. The lunar rhythms affect the cycles in many species, including human beings. Everything under the moon moves. Even mountains move, albeit slowly. Everything in this world is in flux, constantly transforming. Movement is change, and change is in the nature of things. Mother Life renews herself through this.

We live in an ocean of energy, and all energy has consciousness. This ocean is vast, alive and intelligent. We are fields of energy within it, touching and being touched by the energy fields around us. Our thoughts, feelings, actions, and words are like ripples or waves, and everything in the ocean is birthing, growing, transforming, and flowing into everything else. This is the process of evolution.

Sometimes, energy changes gradually, but transformation can also happen suddenly, as in a flash of lightning. Before thunder and lightning occur, the atmosphere is often heavy and sultry. Tension builds until the discharge of electric light and heat clears the atmosphere, arousing fresh vitality. Transformation in us can follow a similar pattern of tension building before a sudden discharge.

Our energy field includes the auric envelope surrounding our body. Everything that happens in each aspect of our Self all the way around the Medicine Wheel affects it. In the opposite direction, path awareness keeps us mindful of our deepest identity, purpose, and direction. When we align ourselves with the evolving truth of who we are, our energy field is bright and vital.

Energy intelligence includes being aware of how energy is moving in us and being able to shift our energy-state to keep it bright. Our energy-state includes our spirit, emotion, body, and mind; when we shift one aspect, we shift all of it. **Change Your Body, Change Your Mind** section explores the power to shift and transform our state.

We also need to be aware of whether our thoughts, words, and actions are life-enhancing or life-diminishing, because they affect our vitality. **Tending the Spirit-Fire** is about learning to be aware of them and to care for our life force. **Judge, Critic, or Observer?** goes further into this theme, because judgement separates us from life and reduces energy consciousness.

We have many voices within us. To have vitality and enthusiasm, we need to listen to their different perspectives. This principle is equally true when we are together in groups. The section called **Have All the Voices Been Heard?** explores the way of council. Through council we can bring the various perspectives into alignment in order for our energy to flourish.

Change Your Body,
Change Your Mind

Consciousness has "field effects." When a nervous person walks into a room, others notice their nervousness, while a person emanating calm, confidence, and light lifts the atmosphere. We affect the field around us, whether we are conscious of it or not. Energy awareness is our ability to read energy in and around us and to affect it with our thoughts, words, and deeds.

This story is about a project I've been working on. It's a project involving young people who face a variety of issues. They may have experienced bullying of different kinds—physical, emotional, or intellectual. Others come from homes that aren't supportive or nurturing. Or they may suffer from racial, gender, or some other form of discrimination. Most of them want more self-confidence and friendship.

The project involves youth workers, mentors, and various instructors. My part in it is to help them gain life skills, such as self-awareness and energy management.

On the first day of the programme, we go to a stable to work with horses. It is a powerful experience for young people, because horses can teach many things, especially about how you affect the energy field around you.

The horse arena we work in is like a huge shed, with soft, sandy stuff underfoot. On this day, Chelsea ventures a nervous hand towards Maverick, but with a toss of the head and a flick of the ears, the horse moves away.

"Why did he back away?" I ask the 14-year-old.

She pauses to reflect and realizes Maverick was responding to her own energy-state.

Giving young people the experience of leading horses helps them see how the inner affects the outer. In the wild, horses are prey animals and, therefore, alert to threats around them. When you approach a horse, you approach a clear mirror that reflects your state of consciousness. If you approach with fear, they will respond to that; approach with confidence and respect, and they will respond to that.

Before meeting the horses, we've shared with our young guests how deep breathing calms and centres you. Now that we're in the arena, we start to coach the young people in meeting the horses with respect.

"You wouldn't want to be treated as an object, and neither would a horse. Like us, horses have feelings and needs. Like us, they want friends."

Learning to get a horse to cooperate makes us use faculties we don't often think about. You can't physically push a horse around or persuade it with reason; it won't understand the nuances of language. Instead, you need to give attention to such things as tone of voice, feeling, and intention, because the horse is listening to your heart and your whole energy field. You need energy awareness.

It isn't only horses that read energy. All animals do, including dogs, wasps, and flies. Humans read energy, but often we do so subconsciously because our attention is occupied with verbal thought. Reading energy is our ability to pick up impressions and notice atmospheres. It is a skill we can deepen and master.

There are many situations where we use this awareness. Actors change their energy to affect the energy of the audience. Teachers use theirs to communicate and command the energy field of their class. Salespeople read the energy of potential customers and then try to adapt conditions to be conducive to a sale. Doctors, therapists, and other professionals read their clients by listening beyond the words. And parents tune into their children's energy to know what they need.

But if energy awareness is a key to our success in many areas, how can we develop it?

I introduce this subject for young people with a drama exercise called Change the Body, Change the Mind. The young people line up in two rows facing each other, and take it in turns to cross over and greet one another. They each do it twice, using two completely contrasting energies. The aim is to demonstrate how you can access different energy states through the body and thought. It works because energy states are composed of all aspects of self—body, mind, emotion, and spirit. If you change one of these, you change all of them.

Let's say, for example, I feel bored or depressed. My body expresses it, and I might be looking down, slouching, and hunching my shoulders. If I deliberately raise my eyes from the ground, straighten up, and move my shoulders back, it changes my energy state. It shifts not only the energy I'm giving to others but also how I'm feeling and thinking. Body language communicates not only to others but also to ourselves.

Changing your thoughts also changes your energy. For example, when you change thought-phrases like *It's hopeless* or *I can't do this* to *I'll give it a go* or *I'm seeking a way to do this*, those thought-phrases have a different effect on your energy state. In the opposite direction of the Medicine Wheel, the Southwest, is managing thought. Managing the activity of our brain has a direct influence on our energy.

Imagining something is a potent form of thought that changes our energy. If you imagine something fearful, you begin to generate fear. Or if you think of spring flowers, tranquil waters, and sunny skies, these thoughts shape your energy field in different ways. And if you want serenity, you could bring up the image of one of the great peacemakers.

Some years ago, I went to an interview for a job teaching English in a language school. I arrived early and having prepared my physical appearance at home, I now prepared my energy. I breathed deeply into each of the energy centres in my body, imagining them becoming clear and bright. I noticed how this affected my vitality—it energized and calmed me. Then I pictured one of the great teachers, an example of centred compassion, courage, and wisdom. Feeling these qualities in my body, mind, and energy field, I then walked into the school.

I don't know how it would have gone if I hadn't prepared my energy like this, but the whole atmosphere of the interview was positive. Almost from the start, I felt an alignment of energy with the people interviewing and was invited to start work soon.

I ask Chelsea: "How could you change your inner state to get a better response from the horse?"

She remembers the deep breathing practice we did earlier and takes a conscious, calming breath. She now approaches Maverick with renewed confidence. This time he doesn't shy away but warms to her touch.

If you want to lead a horse, approach with open sensitivity and allow its energy to join with yours. I have been lucky enough to see Chelsea and many other young people move from timidity to having confidence. And I've seen horses feel so attracted by their energy that they've followed them around obstacles without even a rope attached.

PRACTICE: Vital Breath

This practice develops your vital presence and awareness of energy. Deepening your breath changes your body and shifts your state of energy consciousness. It brings you into a deep, centred presence and a greater alignment with the Universe.

Begin to breathe slowly and steadily. Exhale completely, then inhale to the bottom of your lungs. Feel your lungs expand as the air comes in. As you steadily fill your lungs, imagine light from the Universe flowing into you. Pause for a moment as this energy scintillates through you—cleansing, clarifying, and healing. Then release it back into the Universe.

Direct this beautiful light to each of your energy centres in turn: first to the centre in your sex organs, then to your womb, or ki area, then your solar plexus, heart, throat, forehead, and brain. The eighth breath is into the whole physical body, energizing every cell; the ninth is to the luminous cocoon around the physical body; and the 10th is to the higher Self that extends upwards from the crown of your head.

It is said that much of our breathing is limited to 10–30 percent of our lung capacity. When you vitalize your lungs with oxygen, it courses through your veins, normalizing cortisol levels, building resilience, and toning your vagus nerve. And by directing it into your energy centres with deliberate attention, you activate and align all aspects of your consciousness.

Notice if your posture has changed as a result of this breathing practice. Allow your body to express this new consciousness and power.

Tending the Spirit Fire

Changing energy state by shifting the body or breath maintains our vitality. A second step of energy awareness is learning to feed our life force from within. We can imagine our life force as a fire. How can we care for it and keep it bright?

Let's open this up with a story from the United States: Caroline's healing journey.

Caroline had done really well at a prestigious university on the East Coast. Even among a class of high achievers, her grades had been outstanding. Much was expected of her, and her career in advertising was beginning to take off. She'd already helped secure several good clients and was renting an apartment on the Upper East Side of New York. Her lifestyle pulsed with adrenalin.

But there was a price. Sometimes she'd wake in the middle of the night and sit bolt upright. The next day she'd be tired but wired and have to push through it. Fatigue was stalking her. Then she had a car accident, and her life fell apart.

She was in hospital for weeks. Her nights were filled with nameless dread, her days bewildered by the shock, immobility, and memories of mangled wreckage on the freeway. Gradually, her injuries healed, and she was allowed home. But it felt empty. It wasn't "home" any more.

She was anxious to get back to normal and missed the buzz of texts, meetings, and deadlines, but she felt weak and didn't want to go out. She was sensitive to the smell of traffic. And though she spent more and more time resting, she had little energy.

Christmas came around again, and she was expected at a family gathering. Before her accident she had been very sociable, but now she planned to make her excuses and leave as soon as possible. It was just too much effort to present herself and talk to people.

The party turned out to be better than expected. She had a conversation with her cousin Kim, one of the few relatives she felt she could trust. Kim lived with her husband out West, and they had a cabin in the woods. When she invited Caroline to come and stay for a while, Caroline knew this would be the space to get herself together again.

Even so, it took several months to disentangle from the city and find the energy to make the journey. After her plane landed it was delayed on the runway, and Caroline started talking with the woman in the next seat. She found herself unexpectedly opening up to this stranger and telling the outline of her story. As they parted, the woman introduced herself as "Dr. Wu—Gladys Wu. I'm an energy practitioner."

A week later, she found the woman's card in her pocket. Back in New York, Caroline had tried various therapists and doctors, but without much improvement. She must be desperate to try this. It was probably woo-woo, she thought, especially coming from a person called Wu. But she was also curious, and Kim drove her to an appointment.

At the first session, Gladys gave her an energy treatment, lightly touching her in places and moving her hands a couple of inches away from her body. Caroline drifted into a blissful state filled with light. When she surfaced and opened her eyes, Gladys was smiling.

"Your fire's been low. You need to feed it with the right fuel. Not just things from outside; feed it from within, with powerful thoughts and feelings. I'd like to give you some practices to do," she said.

She told Caroline to go outdoors every day. "Give yourself time to contemplate. Get out in nature and walk in those woods around your place. Breathe the vitality of the pine trees." She also told her to lie face down on the ground and commune with the earth.

"That's the most healing relationship of all."

For the second practice, Dr. Wu got her to start a list of memories of high energy. They needed to involve positive emotions, such as appreciation, joy, or love. Caroline remembered falling in love on holiday in Jamaica, playing with her dog, and designing costumes for her high school drama productions. Then Gladys guided her through an inner practice.

> ***"First, take 10 deep breaths. Allow yourself to relax deeper with each breath.***
>
> ***Now recall this time in Jamaica, the sun on your face, the sand, the sea. Make it real in your imagination. Activate all your inner senses."***

Caroline remembered laughing with her beloved and felt a glow of love inside her.

> ***"Let this feeling expand."***

When the session finished, Caroline felt tears in her eyes, but they were tears of gladness. She agreed to do the practices and come back to see Dr. Wu again. She started "feeding the fire" three times a day. It lifted her mood. Each time she did them, a cascade of positive feelings washed through her.

She liked the metaphor of feeding her inner fire and spent time gazing into the log fire in her cabin. She made a ritual out of gathering sticks for it, thanking the trees, and learning to discern which sticks would burn well. She would grade the wood in different sizes.

It made her think about the fuel she'd been feeding her inner fire. Before the accident, she had fed it with adrenalin, and it had raged. Afterwards her despair and desolation had been like rotten wood that made a smoky fire.

She realized that she'd been withholding love from herself, driving herself onwards with the dream of material status and fear of her parents' disapproval. No, she wasn't going back to New York.

She wasn't going to let civilization shut down her life force again.

She needed to heal; she needed to dream. She'd been making some curtains and doing other sewing jobs for Kim. She'd always been handy with a needle and thread. As a girl, she'd loved playing with fabrics and designing costumes. For now, she'd offer a service mending or altering clothes. People always wanted adjustments on their favourite garments.

She started reading books about positive psychology. They inspired her enough to think of studying the subject formally. But going back to college would be a retrograde step. She wanted to work with clothing but knew this would not be in mainstream fashion. Eventually, she found an opportunity to design costumes for a theatre company and moved to Portland to take it up.

Caroline learned to feed her vitality from within. In mainstream culture, we value outward achievement over inner contentment— becoming before being. But if we're going to maintain our balance and send ripples of balanced energy into the world, we need to give attention to the vitality of our life force. We can't assume that our spirit-fire will tend itself.

Thoughts of self-judgement and low self-esteem are like putting damp, rotten wood on your fire. Overstimulation is putting too much wood on all at once. Being stuck in routine is not putting enough on. But feeding it with just the right amount of dry fuel is respecting your Self as a sacred being. Then your beauty and excellence shine.

PRACTICE: Feeding the Fire

A way to feed your energy from within is by calling forward vital, life-enhancing images. First, go into a state of relaxation using the breath. Second, use memory and imagination to evoke positive feelings. Then affirm these feelings to yourself in words. And lastly, count yourself back to full waking consciousness.

Find a place where you can be uninterrupted for five minutes. Close your eyes and relax. Take 10 deep breaths, releasing tension and dropping deeper with each breath.

Bring to mind something that makes you happy. It could be a memory, something you imagine, or a combination. It could be a person, group, animal, or activity—anything that gives you a feeling of happiness. Imagine it in as much detail as possible, using your inner senses. Make it real.

Notice how happiness feels. Let this feeling grow stronger. Allow it to cascade into every cell, synapse, and sinew. Now say aloud to yourself "I am happy" 10 times. Count down from 10 to 1, smile, and open your eyes.

You can do this with any expansive emotion such as appreciation, serenity, or love. Adapt the affirmation accordingly; for example, "I am love."

I learned this practice from Billy Mills and deeply appreciate him for it. He is a charity worker who has done a lot to help people improve their lives, partly with teachings inherited from his Lakota ancestors.[24]

Judge, Critic, or Observer?

Life-enhancing thought boosts vitality: life-diminishing thought reduces it, and one of our most prevalent life-diminishing thought-patterns is judgement. In essence, it divides us from life and withholds the flow of love from Self and others.

Let's take Salem, Massachusetts, in the 1690s as an example. It is notorious for the hunting of witches and shows how rumour, superstition, and fanaticism can take over the collective mind of a society.

What happened was that children and young women started having fits and strange symptoms. This triggered a frenzy of fear. It was thought to be the work of the devil and various women were accused of acting as his agents. Nineteen were executed, one was tortured to death, and four more died in prison.

What caused this collective delirium? And what does this episode reflect about our own society?

The Puritans left the Old World for the New in order to practise their religion unhindered. They believed in original sin, the idea that humans are inherently flawed. They also believed in redemption—in saving themselves from everlasting damnation through extreme piety and conquering any "depraved" urges. Toys and games were banned, dance and music forbidden, apart from unaccompanied singing of hymns. Boys were punished for strong emotions; girls were repressed for being girls. Women were thought to be especially dangerous because they could tempt men into sin.

In the history of humanity's bad ideas, original sin is outstanding. It is a carcinogenic concept, a disease deleterious to human happiness, a pernicious perversity that's caused colossal conflict in the human soul. Even in secular cultures today, some of us have been insidiously haunted by its ghost, carrying a sense of shame or guilt deep in the subconscious. But extreme puritanism promoted the fear that any kind of pleasure, happiness, or self-esteem could trap you into the clutches of the devil.

And it was difficult to challenge this paradigm. No questions were allowed; it was claimed that if you denied the existence of demons, you denied God.

Fanaticism doesn't depend on original sin for its belief structure; it can get behind any ideology. It's a state of consciousness, and history offers many examples—the Inquisition, the Nazis, and so on.

But these are the "olds;" what of the "news"? A sample of recent atrocities includes child abuse of various kinds—abduction, slaughter, and teaching children to kill—and terror attacks on cities. Typically, we hear about these events with shock, outrage, and fear. We feel polarized into "us versus them." But fanaticism and terrorism are ultimately problems of consciousness. What is really needed to heal and transform them?

It helps to understand the energies that need to be transformed. We can best understand them by studying them in ourselves.

It's easy to become bigoted towards bigots. Bigotry is infectious; it's like a disease in that it's not a state of ease or peace. But how can we heal ourselves and develop immunity? One response that doesn't work is trying to out-bigot the bigot. As Gandhi is said to have observed: "An eye for an eye and the whole world goes blind." A judgement for a judgement, and the whole field gets polarized.

Winston Churchill said: "A fanatic is one who can't change his mind and won't change the subject." The mind of the fanatic is an extreme form of judgement; a way of thinking that divides the Universe into black and white, good and bad, right and wrong. Judgement sees the Self or others as fundamentally flawed—in some way not enough.

There is a distinction between judgement in the sense of condemnation and discernment. We need to discern between what is life-enhancing and what is life-diminishing, between being aligned or distorted. Everyone goes into distortion at times, but it doesn't mean we're essentially depraved or bad. And while we may need to take a stand against some actions—our own or others'—we don't need to condemn the person. Everyone makes mistakes, but none of us need be condemned for them. Mistakes are opportunities to learn something, and discernment helps us see the learning much better than self-judgement.

Another distinction is between judge and critic. A critic doesn't have to be judgemental. We need to look in the mirror of life in order to learn and grow.

Without the reflection of criticism and challenge, we may fall into fanaticism.

Judgement is an ego trip. The essence of ego is separation; the essence of judgement is withholding love. Judging others as "wrong" gives the ego a feeling of status by making it "right," but it also isolates us from true presence and deep relationship. It closes the door to the centre of the Self. When we believe that we're so right and they're so wrong that we're allowed to do anything, the fanatic has taken over our mind.

We also need to look at our beliefs and reconsider the belief-structures that underpin our experience. Is there really an "us and them," or only an "us"? Is this a black-and-white Universe divided into good and bad? If you accept the premise that each of us is in Self-authority, we have choice about what we believe. But whatever we believe affects our energy, consciousness, and experience. If we see the Universe divided, the Self will be divided. If we see the Universe as one, the Self will feel one.

In Shakespeare's play, Hamlet says: "There is nothing either good or bad but thinking makes it so." [25] When the mind goes into stillness and we stop thinking, we experience the world as whole again. Through deep presence, we connect with our Self-Essence and with the essence in all things and people. The essence is neither good nor bad; it is the centre.

How can we heal ourselves of judgement? A first step is to practice deepening our present moment awareness and connection with source. This expands our awareness so that we're more able to notice any judgements of self or others as they arise. Then we can simply smile at these thoughts and let them go. There is no need to judge ourselves. We're on a learning journey in life and can accept ourselves, even when we make mistakes, even for the worst things we've ever done. Paradoxically, accepting ourselves enables us to change.

And we need to change our thoughts when we notice that we're judging others. As Jesus put it: "Judge not, lest you be judged." [26] Why judge others for their accent, hairdo, or mistakes? They're simply doing the best they can at the level of consciousness they've reached. That doesn't mean we can't challenge them, but we can do so lovingly, holding in mind their unlimited potential.

Perhaps we needed the experience of separation on our long journey of evolution. But now it's time to move towards oneness and to accept that the Divine is within each of us.

PRACTICE: Appreciation

Presence is an antidote to judgement. Deep presence connects you with the unity behind creation and brings you into appreciation, a profound openness to the value of things as they are.

In the first part of this practice, consider things of beauty and pleasure. Savour them one by one: a baby's smile, a bunch of flowers, great music, the sunset. Feel the perfection of what's in your life, and feel thankful for it. Fill your energy field with the endorphins of gratitude.

Extend this feeling towards yourself. Appreciate that you are a unique expression of universal life force. Count the gifts that life has given you: your creative spirit, senses, and feelings; your ability to love, laugh, and learn; and so on. Notice all this abundance with gratitude. Appreciate all that you are, even including the areas where you know you need to grow.

Let this contemplation take you into an expanded state of consciousness. From this state, contemplate something that challenges and troubles you. It could be a conflict, a lack, or a loss. Without denying how you have felt about it, don't get caught up in those feelings this time. Be unattached. Look for something you can appreciate about it. Is there any opportunity here?

For example, you might look for how you could empower yourself or learn from this challenge. This is a way of making peace with your life and reducing stress, as well as expanding consciousness, and it may enable you to meet the challenge in more wholeness.

Appreciation expands your awareness and opens the heart wider. It takes you beyond ordinary thinking. It has been called "the Self's most powerful ally."

Have All the Voices
Been Heard?

Groups of people thrive when all their voices are heard. The collective energy retains vitality when all the viewpoints are expressed and honoured. This calls for integrity and deep, respectful listening.

I'm standing in the shade of a great tree. Its trunk is so thick that to encircle it would need several people holding hands with outstretched arms. It's not that tall, as trees go, but its canopy is dark and aromatic. It's a venerable yew of great age, and I am full of awe and reverence, knowing that its estimated age is over 2,500 years old. It was already growing when Buddha, Confucius, and Socrates walked the Earth, and this land would have been a quiet island in the River Thames, its peace not shattered by the roar of planes from nearby Heathrow airport, as it is now.

And this is not any old tree.

It was around here, in the summer of 1215, that King John and his barons met to parley. This area had long been a place for people to council together. Its name, Runnymede, means "meadow of the runes," because the Anglo-Saxons would consult the oracle of the runes before holding council here. And it was probably under this ancient tree that the king and barons agreed Magna Carta.

The Magna Carta, or Great Charter, is an inky parchment written in a language few people now understand, but it is kept with reverence. It symbolizes the principle that no one is above the law; that is, you can't make up the rules as you go along.

210

The tradition of Magna Carta is itself like a tree that has borne fruit in many lands. Many branches have grown from its trunk, among them free speech, restorative justice, and the principle of no imprisonment without fair trial. But what does it signify for the awakening of humanity's consciousness?

It represents the opening of conditions conducive to our collective awakening. It's not that these conditions never existed before, nor that there weren't highly evolved spiritual cultures earlier in the long walk of humanity—Ancient India, Mexico, or parts of Polynesia, for example. But the Magna Carta symbolized the sowing of a seed of potential for the whole of our species to evolve to the next level of consciousness.

The right to free speech is an aspect of this potential. Behind free speech stand free thought and free enquiry; the freedom to question opens us to fresh insight and to the unlimited potential of spirit.

Another aspect of this potential is the recognition of the right of peoples to make collective agreements (laws), and for these agreements to be honoured until such time as the people agree to change them.

Such agreements come about as a result of council. Council depends on deep listening and the respect that each person comes to council in self-authority. So the tradition of Magna Carta offers the potential for societies to evolve into ones based on personal power rather than power over others.

The ground for any relationship to flourish—whether it's a relationship between two people or a community relationship at local, national, or international level—is clear, conscious agreement. Clear agreements with others emerge from the clarity of agreements we make with our Self. This allows us to bring our wholeness of heart to agreements.

Council offers the potential for agreement to emerge. Of course, there are many times when people don't agree, but through council they can at least agree to disagree. And when full-hearted agreement does emerge, it enables people's energy to flower together.

One elder said: "We each have one point of view, but Great Spirit has many viewing points." Every person has a unique perspective, but when we respect our diversity, it opens us to greater wholeness. Deep and respectful listening is thus a vital part of council, and all the many forms of council that have evolved on every continent have that in common.

King John and countless others sought to exercise absolute authority and power over others in systems of dictatorship. These systems make it harder for the human spirit to learn and grow through self-authority and self-responsibility. Magna Carta enabled the evolution of governance through formal dialogue between government and opposition. This is adversarial politics, which generally allows more freedom of thought and inquiry. But there are yet more steps for us to take, and the Way of Council offers the potential to find our way.

This is holistic politics based on the circle. One way of council I have studied—the Earth Wisdom Council—uses the form of the Medicine Wheel. Each of the eight directions is represented by both a woman and a man who speak from that perspective. So it is designed to care for balance, wholeness, and the wellbeing of the whole community. I have witnessed various circles of people use it to access their collective wisdom on particular questions.

It may be difficult to imagine doing politics other than through parties, compromise, and majority vote. But the Earth Wisdom Council is inclusive, allows all the voices to be heard, and enables decision-making through consensus. It calls us to a different mindset, a heightened aware-ness of relationship with all things in the inner and outer Universe. And it calls for a high level of sincerity in those who stand to speak for the whole community. We need to work on ourselves to become clear elders for the community.

While musing under the ancient yew at Runnymede, I remember the story of another tree: the Great Tree of Peace of the Iroquois Confederacy. It may have been earlier than Magna Carta that five Native tribes formed a league—the Iroquois Confederacy—at the foot of a great tree in what is now upstate New York.

They had been warring for centuries—the Mohawk, Seneca, Oneidas, Cayuga, and Onondaga. Then Hiawatha and a man those tribes refer to as The Peacemaker travelled around the various villages, calling the five peoples together. They ceremonially overturned a large tree and buried their weapons in the hollow, giving rise to the phrase "bury the hatchet." Then they replanted the tree and set an eagle at the top to watch for any dangers.

To this day, the Iroquois govern themselves through a system of councils designed to produce holistic and balanced decisions. Their democracy inspired Benjamin Franklin and other Founding Fathers of the United States.

Every society has the challenge of balancing the rights of the individual with the needs of the collective. Some societies bury the individual under the state; others are so individualistic they neglect the common good. Yet we humans thrive when there is a balance between the freedom to express our uniqueness and the togetherness of supportive relationship. And the way of council provides structure for these twin forces—individuality within togetherness—to come into dynamic balance.

The eagle on top of the tree symbolizes the clear sight and vigilance needed to maintain peace, liberty, and the balance of individuality within togetherness. The eagle is alert for potential conflict. Without this alertness, without the deep listening vital for all the people's voices to be heard, without the sincerity of spirit of those who weave and care for the vital fabric of democracy, neither the commonwealth nor the individual spirits who create it can flourish.

There have been many times when we have neglected the ancient tree and allowed its fruits to shrivel on its branches. But the old tree is redolent with the irrepressible yearning of the human spirit: our urge for freedom, truth, and beauty. This will never die.

PRACTICE: The Way of Council

This practice can be used either in relationship with others or within your Self. It is a way to access the collective genius of the group or your own inner wisdom. In both situations it leads to alignment, and alignment allows energy to flower.

In groups there are sometimes voices that remain silent. Until they are heard the energies behind them may block the group energy from moving forward. We can enable them to be expressed by creating a sacred container. Everyone has the right to be heard, just as they have the right to remain silent.

To create such a container, invite people to sit in a circle, ideally so that everyone can see everyone else. Place something beautiful in the centre, such as a vase of flowers or a candle. The essence of this way of council is deep listening; ask people for agreement to listen respectfully without judgement or interruption. Establish a tone of receptivity and safety.

Pass a talking stick or other object around the circle to signify whose turn it is to speak. Let each person have an opportunity to speak what needs to be spoken. Ask them to speak of their own experience—to speak from "I," not "you." For some people, it may be enough to hold the talking stick or object for a moment and then pass it on.

Hearing each other's voices in community builds understanding. It is a way to gather the collective wisdom and may lead to agreement.

It's also important to create an energy container when you listen to your internal voices. This could mean bringing beauty into your physical surroundings, but certainly means coming with the centre of your Self and connecting with the Universe. Listen to yourself without judgement.

There may be voices within that carry worry or doubt. When you listen to their message, you see what is needed to move forward in integrity. Also listen to the voices of each of the eight energies of the Medicine Wheel. Practise looking at your situation through each of these perspectives.

Awakening Our Whole Circle of Self

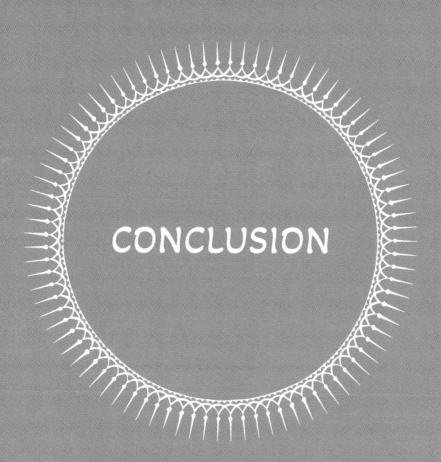

CONCLUSION

The Centre of the Self

In chapter one, we opened with the question of how to reawaken our relationship with the one light? We explored peak experiences and saw that many things can trigger them. Now having journeyed around the Medicine Wheel, we come to the centre of the Self, which is the source of peak experiences.

This centre is the formless in which all forms exist. It is the Divine, the home of our vital Self-Essence, and the source of our self-authority. It is everywhere. It is the "I" that paradoxically has nothing but gives us everything. Without it, we would not exist. It is the core light through which we experience epiphany.

Astronaut Edgar Mitchell experienced epiphany looking through the window of his *Apollo* space capsule. He had the "breathtaking experience of seeing planet Earth floating in the immensity of space—the incredible beauty of a splendid blue-and-white jewel floating in the vast, black sky." He felt the numinous presence of the Divine. But then his thoughts turned to people's behaviour in daily life: our aggression and violence, lying and cheating, lust and greed. He considered our abuse of water, land and air, our wars, bigotry and intolerance. "As I survey the challenge facing humanity today," he wrote, "I see only one answer: a transformation of consciousness." [27]

Pictures of Mother Earth were brought back by the Apollo astronauts and used on many posters in the 1970s when I was a student. This image of our planet inspired an epiphany I had at that time.

It was a beautiful day in early summer, and I'd been studying intensely for exams. Now I had time to go for a walk in the countryside with my friend Duncan. We enjoyed the flowers, the flying insects, and the smell of the grass, and as we came home late in the day, the evening light on the trees. We sensed that everything in nature was in harmony. That night as I lay waiting for sleep to enfold me in her arms, I noticed a sensation in my solar plexus. Perhaps because of the deep wellbeing I'd derived from the day, I stayed with the feeling without labelling it. As I did so, I saw a wheel of fire whirling round, a ring of light spinning like a firework. I focused on this image, and a thought came to me: *Everyone has their own mantra. This is yours. Just meditate on it.*

I concentrated on the image and sensation, and instead of going into ordinary sleep, I was inspired by another realization. Behind the apparent differences with my fellow students, each of us pursuing qualifications in different fields, there was something the same in all of us. I didn't have words for this. I simply had the feeling that under the surface we were all one, that all of us were the same in essence. And in that moment, I knew that nothing was wrong; everything was as it should be. This awareness energized and elated me, and when I surfaced in the morning, I felt the same clarity and brightness I used to feel when waking up as a child.

This mystical state of consciousness lasted for the next three weeks. I didn't engage in my usual concerns or ordinary thoughts but was intensely present. I didn't attend to my studies; they didn't seem important in the light of the awareness that we are one. There was no need to seek knowledge in books, because I felt all wisdom was already in me. I simply needed to access it.

We usually "re-source" ourselves in deep sleep when we're at one with Source. We can also resource ourselves by being intensely present, because that too is a state of oneness with Source. So I found I had plenty of energy, even though I wasn't sleeping normally. At night, I would lie down and concentrate on the feeling of my body. I felt my oneness with Earth. I thought of Earth as you see her from space—an orb of beauty shimmering in the darkness. Somebody had spoken to me of "universal mind"—I knew the truth of that phrase and was at one with a mind far greater than my individuality. I felt the truth of One World. This was my religion, I thought: *One World.* Suddenly, my reality was grander than it had been.

Before this, I hadn't thought about visionary experiences or spiritual training. I hadn't considered an inner journey to explore the Self, because I didn't know we had a Self to explore. But we are multidimensional beings, and I experienced a sudden eruption of consciousness from deep inside. It inspired my journey of self-knowledge, and years later I found language to describe what had happened. In Buddhism, it would be called an "experience of nirvana;" in Hinduism, the centre of the Self would be called the Atman, or universal soul.

In this time of global crisis, we are called to make the next step of evolution. We need to ask what we need for a collective epiphany and transformation of consciousness.

Human consciousness is complex, and whether we believe such a transformation is possible depends on the aperture of our state of consciousness. The Medicine Wheel is a map for our journey of opening this possibility. It enables us to expand our perspective of who we are and our relationship with all the energies of life.

As we face the rising sun in the East, we realize that we are the light of universal life force. In the Southeast, we increase our awareness of the infinite, ever-present Mystery. In the South, we experience wholeness by embracing the endless diversity of forms. We turn to the Southwest and remember the deep truth of who we are and our sacred path of awakening in this holy dream. To the West, we honour the healing power of sacred Grandmother Earth and our body-temple. In the Northwest, we open to the dreaming Universe and access the power to co-create with our thought, word, and action. Facing the North, we access heightened wisdom through the heart-mind to act for the wellbeing of the whole. And in the Northeast, we tend the spirit fire.

All of these directions are inherent potentials in everyone, and when we align with this full spectrum of life forces, we open the doorway to the sacred centre of the Self. This doorway leads to our transformation, and as more people step through it, our collective field of consciousness shifts.

My last story is about a Lakota visionary and holy man, Black Elk, and the last words will be his.

In the 1930s, an American poet and scholar John Neihardt was researching the history of the Wild West. He was led to meet Black Elk in the Black Hills of South Dakota and interviewed him through an interpreter. The result was his book, *Black Elk Speaks*.

Black Elk had lived through the end of the Lakota living as hunter-gatherers; they had now been settled on reservations. As a young man, he had fought at the Battle of the Little Big Horn and the massacre of Wounded Knee. When Neihardt first met him, the old man answered his questions about history politely but briefly, and it became obvious to Neihardt that there was something else the old man wanted to speak about.

The conversation lapsed into silence. After some moments Black Elk spoke again. He said that soon he would be under the grass and that he felt Neihardt had been sent to save the great vision he had received as a child. It was a vision for all the peoples of the world, and yet Black Elk felt great sadness that he had been unable to manifest it in his own lifetime on Earth.

When he was nine, Black Elk fell into a trance for several days, and his parents feared for his life. During this time, he received the great vision.

In the vision, Black Elk was taken into the clouds and met horses representing the powers of the four directions. He stepped through a rainbow into a teepee where six grandfathers were holding council. They gave him sacred gifts of power and showed him many things, including scenes of great suffering for his people. He danced with the horses, and this brought healing. Then he saw the whole world as one, with the hoops of many nations united in one sacred hoop. At the centre was a great tree that came back into flower. He saw that all people are the children of one father and one mother and that the tree was holy.

There is more detail of the vision in the book *Black Elk Speaks*, but speaking to another writer Black Elk said this:

The first peace, which is the most important, is that which comes in the souls of people when they know their relationship, their oneness, with the Universe and all its powers, and when they know that at the centre of the Universe dwells Wakan-Tanka, the great spirit, and that this centre is everywhere and within all of them. The second peace is that which is made between two people, and the third between nations. But above all, you must understand there will never be peace between nations until there is first known that first peace, which is in the souls of people.[28]

Blessings on each and every one of us, as we evolve our consciousness and create a world of peace, unconditional love, and wholeness in diversity.

We Are Spirits of Light in Human Form

Notes

1. Albert Einstein, "Letter to Robert S. Marcus, February 12, 1950" in *Einstein and the Rabbi: Searching for the Soul* (New York: Flatiron Books, 2018). Marcus was grieving the death of his son.

2. Jalaluddin Rumi, *The Mathnawi of Jalaluddin Rumi* (Konya, Turkey: Konya Metropolitan Municipality, 2004, first published in 1273).

3. Fred Alan Wolf, *Time Loops and Space Twists: How God Created the Universe*, (San Antonio, TX: Hierophant Publishing, 2011).

4. Mary Shelley, *Frankenstein* (Ballingslov, Sweden: Wisehouse Classics; 2nd Revised 1831 ed., 2015).

5. Peter Jackson's film, *The Fellowship of the Rings* (2001). Not mentioned in Tolkien's book.

6. Lewis Carroll, *Alice's Adventures in Wonderland* (London: MacMillan, 1865).

7. William Blake, *Auguries of Innocence* (London, CreateSpace, 2014, first published by Blake in 1803).

8. A. A. Milne, *The House at Pooh Corner* (London: Methuen, 1928).

9. Shunryu Suzuki, *Zen Mind, Beginner's Mind: Informal Talks on Zen Meditation and Practice* (Boulder, CO: Shambhala, 2011, first published in 1970).

10. A. A. Milne, *Winnie the Pooh* (New York: Dutton, 2017, first published in 1926).

11. Desmond Tutu, *No Future without Forgiveness* (Image/Random House, 2000, first published in 1999).

12. Chuang Tse or Zhuangzi

13. Candace B. Pert, *Molecules of Emotion: The Science behind Mind-Body Medicine* (Simon & Schuster, 1999).

14. Norman Doidge, *The Brain that Changes Itself: Stories of Personal Triumph from the Frontiers of Brain Science* (London, Penguin Life, 2007).

15. C. G. Jung, *Memories Dreams, Reflections* (New York: Vintage, 1989, first published in 1963).

16. From the *Poetic Edda,* a collection of Norse poems (probably 10th century).

17. Max Planck, *"Das Wesen der Materie" ["The Nature of Matter"],* speech in Florence, Italy (1944).

18. Ann Faraday, *The Dream Game* (New York, Harper & Row, 1990, first published in 1975).

19. J. B. Priestley, *Rain Upon Godshill* (NewYork: Harper & Bros., 1939).

20. William Shakespeare, *Measure for Measure,* Act 1, Scene 5.

21. *Mundaka Upanishad* (Advaita Ashrama, 3rd ed, 2000), ch. 3, 1:3.

22. Mohandas K. Gandhi, *On God,* recorded in 1931 by Columbia Gramophone Company while Ghandi was visiting Britain.

23. Leo Tolstoy, *A Letter to a Hindu: 2021 Translation* (Westfall, 2021, first published in 1908).

24. Billy Mills with Nicholas Sparks, *Wokini: Your Personal Journey to Happiness and Self-Understanding (*Quincy, CA: Feather Publishing, 1990).

25. William Shakespeare, *Hamlet,* Act II, Scene 2.

26. Matthew 7:1.

27. Edgar Mitchell, *From Outer Space to Inner Space: An Apollo Astronaut's Journey through the Material and Mystical Worlds* (Newburyport, MA: New Page Books/RedWheel Weiser, 2023, first published in 1996).

28. John Epes Brown, *The Sacred Pipe: Black Elk's Account of the Seven Rites of the Oglala Sioux, The Civilization of the American Indian Series, Vol.36* (Norman, OK: University of Oklahoma Press, 1989).

Bibliography

Blake, William. *Auguries of Innocence*. London: CreateSpace, 2014, first published by Blake in 1803.

Brown, John Epes. *The Sacred Pipe: Black Elk's Account of the Seven Rites of the Oglala Sioux, The Civilization of the American Indian Series, Vol.36*. Norman, OK: University of Oklahoma Press, 1989.

Carroll, Lewis. *Alice's Adventures in Wonderland*. London: MacMillan,1865.

Crawford, Jackson (translator). *The Poetic Edda: Stories of the Norse Gods and Heroes*. Indianapolis, IN: Hackett Classics, 2015.

Doidge, Norman. *The Brain that Changes Itself: Stories of Personal Triumph from the Frontiers of Brain Science*. London: Penguin Life, 2007.

Easwaran, Eknath (translator). *The Upanishads*. Tomales, CA: Nilgiri Press, 2007.

Einstein, Albert. "Letter to Robert S. Marcus, February 12, 1950" in *Einstein and the Rabbi: Searching for the Soul*. New York: Flatiron Books, 2018.

Faraday, Ann. *The Dream Game*. New York: Harper & Row, 1990, first published 1975.

Gandhi, M. K. *An Autobiography or The story of My Experiments with Truth*. London: Penguin, 2001, first published 1929.

Jung, C. G. *Memories, Dreams, Reflections*. New York: Vintage, 1989, first published 1962.

Mills, Billy, with Nicholas Sparks. *Wokini: Your Personal Journey to Happiness and Self-Understanding*. Quincy, CA: Feather Publishing, 1990.

Milne, A. A. *Winnie-the Pooh*. New York: HarperCollins, 2016, first published 1926.

_____. *The House at Pooh Corner*. New York: HarperCollins, 2016, first published 1928.

Mitchell, Edgar. *From Outer Space to Inner Space: An Apollo Astronaut's Journey through the Material and Mystical Worlds*. Newburyport, MA: New Page Books/RedWheel Weiser, 2023, first published in 1996.

Neihardt, John. *Black Elk Speaks.* Complete Ed. Lincoln, NE: Bison Books/University of Nebraska Press, 2014, first published 1926.

Nicholson, R.A. (translator). *The Masnavi I Ma'navi of Rumi: Complete 6 Books.* Oxford: Oxford University Press, 2008, first published 1925–1940.

Pert, Candace B. *Molecules of Emotion: The Science behind Mind-Body Medicine.* New York: Simon & Schuster, 1999.

Planck, Max. *"Das Wesen der Materie"* *["The Nature of Matter"]*, speech in Florence, Italy, 1944.

Priestley, J. B. *Rain Upon Godshill.* NewYork: Harper & Bros., 1939.

Shakespeare, William. *Measure for Measure.* (The Arden Shakespeare). London: Bloomsbury Publishing, 2020.

_____. *Hamlet, Prince of Denmark.* (The Arden Shakespeare). London: Bloomsbury Publishing, 2016.

Shelley, Mary. *Frankenstein.* Ballingslov, Sweden: Wisehouse Classics; 2nd Revised 1831 ed., 2015, first published 1818.

Suzuki, Shunryu. *Zen Mind, Beginner's Mind: Informal Talks on Zen Meditation and Practice.* Boulder, CO: Shambhala, 2011, first published in 1970.

Tolstoy, Leo. *A Letter to a Hindu: 2021 Translation.* Portland OR: Westfall, 2021, first published in 1908.

Tutu, Desmond. *No Future without Forgiveness.* New York: Image/Random House, 2000, first published in 1999.

Wolf, Fred Alan. *Time Loops and Space Twists: How God Created the Universe.* San Antonio, TX: Hierophant Publishing, 2011.

List of Practices

Recommended Connections

https://angele.art

Angele inspires beauty and balance through her art, of which the frontispiece for this book is an example. She trained as a thangka and classical painter and offers prayer paintings.

https://evocativeleadershipmastery.com

Evocative Leadership Mastery is an amazing journey of expanding consciousness. It enables us to be agents of real collective transformation and shape the future for generations to come.

https://imaginalcollective.eco

Imaginal Collective is a growing global community dedicated to inspiring conscious relationship with Self, life, and Earth.

https://northerndrum.com

A UK-based school for Earth-based spirituality and disciplined shamanic practice.

www.carlosphilipglover.com

My own website dedicated to inspiring the healing and transformation of our consciousness.

Acknowledgements

I'd like to honour the many people who've made this book possible: first of all, the Earth Wisdom teachers who've inspired and guided me, and for whom my admiration and gratitude is almost ineffable: WE and RH of Ehama Institute and WtE of Dancehammers; also for the whole lineage of wise and courageous chiefs who went before them.

I salute all my other teachers, including Joseph Rael, Leo Rutherford, and Nick Twilley; Jean-Claude, Arlene, and others of the Process Work School; Sensei John Stoner and the Ki Federation; Chris Luttichau of Northern Drum. There are many more. It was Roshi Joan Halifax, head teacher at Upaya Institute in Santa Fe, who initiated me into earth-based spirituality and told me that anyone, even the lowliest beggar, could be my teacher. I appreciate all the many sisters and brothers of my community and the many stars of consciousness with whom I've sat in circles over the years. When I think of all the people who've taught and touched my life they feel as numerous as the stars. Thank you.

I don't want to forget the non-human helpers. Words emerged as I communed with Clouds, Sky, Trees, and River. Honour to Earth, Air, Fire, and Water in all your expressions.

Thanks to my wonderful parents and ancestor spirits.

More specifically, I acknowledge the love and encouragement of friends like Richard Good. I still have the £20 note he gave me for a copy of this book a good few years ago, and I owe him some change. Many others also helped midwife this baby into the world: my brothers— Simon, Massimo, Jason, Jono, Olly, and Chris; Angele Camus and the beauty that flowed through her heart, hand, and paintbrush onto the book cover; Marta Cisneros, for her incredible generosity and willingness to translate this into Spanish; Shuna Meade, for copy editing; Massimo Giannuzzi, for his technomancy; and Rick Lawrence, for help with graphics and publishing.

My wise, courageous, and beautiful wife Sue has given me the most generous support imaginable. I couldn't have written this without her patience, insights, and loving challenge or her encouragement to follow my heart. I've learned such a lot from being on the journey of intimate relationship with her. We share a passion for the evolution of human consciousness and many interests, including sacred sites. It was her idea to bless the first draft of the book at the Temple of Artemis in Ephesus while on holiday. There among the ancient ruins we asked for blessing from the Goddess and from the Great Mystery.

About the Author

Photo by Chris Smith

Carlos felt the power of Indigenous teachings while living in the Andes in the early 1980s. He canoed into the Amazon and felt deep sorrow about the ecocide caused by oil exploration and cattle ranching. After returning to the UK, he campaigned with Friends of the Earth, particularly on rainforests and climate change. He also explored various paths of self-knowledge, including Theravada Buddhism and Process Oriented Psychology.

These two strands—inner development and outer activism—led him to a question: What is needed for us humans to live in harmony with ourselves and our planet?

He found an answer in the Earth Wisdom Teachings that flourished among the Maya and Toltec and believes the Medicine Wheel has the power to influence and benefit our collective destiny. His teacher told him: "Breathe these teachings into the world. It is time, and maybe some good will come of it." He has since dedicated much of his life to sharing Earth Wisdom with interested people.

Carlos is called "Diamond Light" in Medicine ceremonies. He is the Dance Chief of the annual Drum Dance and holds vision quests, seasonal ceremonies, and learning journeys. He is also guiding the Evocative Leadership Mastery journey in Spain. He lives with his wife in Devon, England.

For more information visit: **www.carlosphilipglover.com**

Index

FINDHORN PRESS

Life-Changing Books

Learn more about us and our books at

www.findhornpress.com

For information on the Findhorn Foundation:

www.findhorn.org

Scan the QR code and save 25% at InnerTraditions.com.
Browse over 2,000 titles on spirituality, the occult, ancient
mysteries, new science, holistic health, and natural medicine.